THE EXPANSION OF
CHRISTIANITY

The Expansion of Christianity

Timothy Yates

InterVarsity Press
Downers Grove, Illinois

Baptist missionaries conduct a baptism at San Salvador, Lower Congo in 1907.

Previous pages: San Ignacio Mission, Baja, Mexico.

Page one: A worshipper receives communion from Fr Thomas Lin at Easter Sunday Mass at the Roman Catholic cathedral in Kaifeng, Henan, China in 1981.

InterVarsity Press
P.O. Box 1400, Downers Grove, IL 60515-1426
World Wide Web: www.ivpress.com
E-mail: mail@ivpress.com

ISBN 0-8308-2358-1

Printed and bound in China

Library of Congress Cataloging-in-Publication Data has been requested

P 15 14 13 12 11 10 9 8 7 6 5 4 3 2 1
Y 14 13 12 11 10 09 08 07 06 05 04

Contents

9.06

128665

Introduction

This book attempts to describe how Christianity expanded across the world. It does not claim to be a complete history of the church from AD 1 to AD 2000. It concentrates on pioneers, Peter and Paul in the 1st century, Columba and Aidan in the Celtic period, and on great missionary figures such as Willibrord and Boniface, Francis Xavier and Robert de Nobili, John Eliot and David Brainerd, William Carey, Robert Moffatt and David Livingstone, Mary Slessor and Florence Young to name a selection. The approach taken is geographical, chapters after the first dealing with continents; and chronological, so that some sense of development in each area of the world is presented in a time sequence.

One of the many deficiencies of such a treatment is

Jesuit Cathedral, Pekin (Beijing).

that, with the concentration on expansion, those considerable reverses experienced by the Christian world, most particularly from Islam in the 7th and 8th centuries, have received little coverage. Something that should not be forgotten is that Christian expansion has not been a continual success story. The great historian of Christian expansion, Kenneth Latourette, put forward the so-called wave theory, by which, despite retreat in periods of its history, to his eye each wave of Christianity reached further than the last.

Certainly in the 20th century Christianity became worldwide in the sense that churches were planted in every major ethnic group in the world, leading one archbishop of Canterbury, William Temple, in the 1940s to call this 'the great new fact of our era'. According to the figures in the *World Christian Encyclopedia*, the statistician David Barrett estimates that there are now some 2,000 million Christians in the world, some 33 per cent of the whole world population. Whereas decline has been experienced in Europe, there has been remarkable growth in the continent of Africa in the 20th century, from some 10 million in 1900 to over 200 million in 2000.

For centuries Christianity was quite as much an Asian religion as it was European. The existence of churches in Egypt and in Ethiopia from the earliest times until today is a reminder also that Christianity retained a foothold in Africa even after the collapse of the North African church of Tertullian, Cyprian and Augustine before the assaults of tribes from Europe and the forces of Islam. For our age it is important to describe the roots of Asian and African Christianity in the early centuries before the age of the explorers led to the expansion of Europeanized Christianity after 1500.

CHAPTER 1

The Mediterranean World

Christianity begins with Jesus of Nazareth. In regard to expansion, the Gospels suggest that Jesus himself put strict limits on his own mission. To a non-Jewish woman, he said, 'I was sent only to the lost sheep of the house of Israel' (Matthew 15:24). There are signs, however, that he envisaged wider effects from his mission. For example, in response to the faith of a Roman soldier he was prompted to say, 'people will come from east and west, from north and south, and will eat in the kingdom of God'. He even suggested that non-Jews, Romans and others would become members of God's 'kingdom', to the exclusion of the chosen race of the Old Testament.

Nevertheless, it was not until after the crucifixion and the preaching of the resurrection that Christianity began to grow beyond Jesus' personal following of the 12 apostles, the 72 disciples of his mission and the rest of the movement's adherents of his lifetime. His execution fell in the time of Pontius Pilate's governorship, whom we know from extra-biblical sources to have been governor of Judea during AD 26–36. We do not know the precise date of the crucifixion but AD 30 or 33 have been advanced as likely. Figures such as Jesus' forerunner, John the Baptist, and Pilate himself appear in non-biblical histories such as those of Josephus (AD c. 37–c. 100) or Tacitus (AD c. 55–c. 113).

For the expansion of the church in its early years we

are, however, heavily dependent on Luke, who wrote two volumes, possibly aimed at a representative Roman enquirer given the name of Theophilus (God-beloved), known to us as the Gospel of Luke and the Acts of the Apostles. The second volume took the story of the Christian movement from the mid-30s to the mid-60s of the 1st century, a crucial period of its development.

Whatever subsequent generations have accepted or rejected, the early Christians believed that the crucified Jesus had been raised from death by an act of God. Luke gives us sample speeches, rather in the manner of the great Greek historian, Thucydides, which seek to convey the basic Christian message as he believed it to have been presented. Peter, leader of the apostolic band, in the first account we have of a Christian sermon given to an audience of Jews, emphasized that God had raised the crucified Jesus: 'This Jesus God raised up, and of that all of us are witnesses.' Jesus was the Messiah of Jewish expectation: 'God has made him both Lord and Messiah, this Jesus whom you crucified' (Acts 2:36). Offensive as this message must have been to devout Jews, assembled in Jerusalem to celebrate the Jewish festival of Pentecost, in

Two early historians

John surnamed the Baptist... was a good man and exhorted the Jews to lead righteous lives, to practise justice towards their fellows and piety towards God and so doing to join in baptism... a consecration of the body implying that the soul was cleansed by right behaviour.

JOSEPHUS, *ANTIQUITIES*, 18.117–118

Nero fastened the guilt [for the fire of Rome] and inflicted the most exquisite tortures on a class hated for their abominations, called Christians by the populace. Christus, from whom the name had its origin, suffered the extreme penalty during the reign of Tiberius at the hands of one of our procurators, Pontius Pilate, and a deadly superstition, thus choked for a moment, again broke out not only in Judea, the first source of the evil but also in the City.

TACITUS, *ANNALS*, XV.44.2–8

Wall painting of
Christ as the
Good Shepherd
(from catacomb
of Priscilla in
Rome, 3rd
century).

*'[Luke] first saw
that the new
Israel like the
old was destined
to have its
history and
recognized that
sacred history
must be related
to the history of
the world. The
life of the church
is not to be a
frenzied
proclamation...
but a steady
programme of
expansion
throughout the
world.'*

STEPHEN NEILL,
*A HISTORY OF
CHRISTIAN MISSIONS*

Luke's account 3,000 people became Christians on that
day and were baptized. The emphasis on the resurrection
was to remain central as the movement spread, so that it
featured equally in addressing a sophisticated audience of
Greeks in Athens. The early preachers saw themselves as
'witnesses', people who had first-hand evidence of an act
of God and, in Peter's case, experience of eating and
drinking with the risen Jesus (Acts 10:41).

Luke's programme
For some time in the 30s Christianity remained a sub-sect
of Judaism. Luke recorded that a number of Jewish priests
joined the movement. Nevertheless, in Luke's own
understanding there was to be a programme of expansion.
The risen Christ had told his followers that their witness
to him was to extend from Jerusalem to wider Judea
and Samaria and to the ends of the earth (Acts 1:8).
By far the largest leap for the young movement was from
Jew to non-Jew or Gentile. Luke showed the intermediate
step to the Samaritans, regarded as heretics by orthodox
Jews; and to a Jewish proselyte (convert) and Ethiopian

African, who was a fringe adherent of Judaism (Acts 8). The main emphasis in Acts was to be on the Gentile mission. Luke himself was a Gentile, probably a Syrian. He developed his theme by way of the conversion of Saul of Tarsus, who became Paul, the apostle to the Gentiles, a story told three times in the book as a form of emphasis (Acts 9; 22; 26); and also through the story of Peter and Cornelius, a Roman soldier and centurion, told twice (Acts 10; 11). In this story Luke provided a beginning for Gentiles that was equivalent to what the day of Pentecost had been for Jews – Gentiles too experienced the Holy Spirit as a result of Peter's preaching about Jesus and joined the church by baptism.

If the early part of Acts can be called the acts of Peter, the later chapters are the acts of Paul. Paul's dramatic conversion has been dated as early as AD 34. The story itself reveals that there were already Christians in Syria and Damascus.

There was also a strong enough church in Antioch in Syria for Christians there to be called by that name for the first time (up to then they may have been called only those of 'the Way', as a sub-sect of Judaism [Acts 24:14]). Saul himself, as a former persecutor of Christians, faced the danger that he would still be regarded as an agent provocateur. It took the generosity of spirit of Barnabas, whom Luke tells us was a Jewish Cypriot, to recruit him as a Christian teacher for the growing church. It was from Antioch that what could be called the first 'overseas' mission took place, when Saul and Barnabas were sent by the local church to Cyprus and conducted a preaching tour across the island from Salamis to Paphos.

Paul the missionary

Gradually, Saul, by now 'Paul', replaced Barnabas as the missionary leader: 'Barnabas and Saul' became 'Paul and Barnabas'. Paul appeared to have a definite strategy as he moved around the Mediterranean world. Many upright Gentiles, represented in Luke's writings by the Ethiopian treasurer and the Roman centurion Cornelius, were

'I was travelling to Damascus with the authority and commission of the chief priests, when at midday along the road... I saw a light from heaven, brighter than the sun, shining around me and my companions. When we had all fallen to the ground, I heard a voice saying to me in the Hebrew language, "Saul, Saul, why are you persecuting me? It hurts you to kick against the goads." I asked, "Who are you, Lord?" The Lord answered, "I am Jesus whom you are persecuting."'

PAUL BEFORE
KING AGRIPPA,
ACTS 26:12–15

attracted by the high moral standards and teaching of the Jewish synagogues and religion. This Gentile fringe, already instructed in the Jewish scriptures of the Old Testament, provided Paul with a natural platform for the Christian gospel. Paul would visit the synagogues of the Jewish dispersion as a first point of entry, as at the other Antioch in Pisidia in modern Turkey and nearby Iconium. Luke showed that this resulted ultimately in hostility from the Jewish communities but also that, as at Iconium, 'a great number of both Jews and Greeks' became Christians.

Through the 40s and 50s, Paul spent much time as an itinerant Christian preacher, teacher and leader. An

The Conversion of St Paul by Caravaggio.

important point of departure was his decision, which Luke attributes to the Holy Spirit and a dream or vision of a Greek man from Macedonia, to cross over to mainland Europe rather than pursue his mission to northern Turkey. In Greece he went from Philippi, the town named after Alexander the Great's father, to Thessalonica and then to Athens and Corinth. We know from his first letter to the Thessalonian Christians (which vies with Galatians as his earliest letter), written probably in AD 49, that his preaching to these Greeks called on them to give up the worship of idols in order to serve instead 'the living and true God' and his Son Jesus 'whom he raised from the dead' (1 Thessalonians 1:9–10). Christianity challenged the polytheism of the ancient world, whether Zeus (Jupiter) and Hermes (Mercury) at Lystra or the goddess Artemis (Diana) at Ephesus.

In Corinth Paul appeared before the Roman proconsul, Gallio, which enables us to date his visit through the evidence of an inscription to AD 51. His work in the Mediterranean world, which included lengthy spells in Corinth of 18 months and in Ephesus of two years, ended with imprisonment in Caesarea and an appeal to Rome, the result both of Jewish hostility and his preference for Roman justice.

By then, however, the emperor was Nero, who was to blame the fire of Rome on Christians in AD 64. By tradition, both Peter and Paul were executed in Rome in the 60s although Acts leaves Paul under house arrest in Rome over a two-year period, apparently free to receive visitors and 'teaching about the Lord Jesus with all boldness and without hindrance' (Acts 28:31). His own letter to the Roman Christians, written in the mid-50s, had given evidence of the size of the Roman church by that time and set out his most comprehensive version of Christianity, and also his hope (probably unrealized) of visiting Spain to preach the gospel as the culminating point of his Mediterranean mission (Romans 15:23).

Bust of Nero
c. AD 54–68

Pliny and Trajan in correspondence

It is my custom, lord emperor, to refer to you all questions where I am in doubt... this is the course I have taken with those who are accused before me as Christians. I asked them whether they were Christians and if they confess I asked them a second and third time with threats of punishment. If they kept to it, I ordered them for execution; for I held no question that whatever it was they admitted in any case obstinacy and unbending perversity deserved to be punished.

PLINY TO TRAJAN

You have adopted the proper course, my dear Secundus, in your examination of the cases of those who are accused to you as Christians, for indeed nothing can be laid down as a general ruling... they are not to be sought out: but if they are accused and convicted, they must be punished – yet on this condition, that whoever declares himself to be a Christian... shall obtain pardon on his repentance however suspicious his past conduct may be.

TRAJAN TO PLINY c. AD 112

'May I have joy of the beasts that are prepared for me... I will even entice them to devour me promptly... now I am beginning to be a disciple. May nothing of things visible or invisible seek to allure me, that I may attain to Jesus Christ.'

IGNATIUS, *LETTER TO THE ROMANS*, V

Rome and persecution

Between Luke's account, which effectively takes the spread of Christianity from Jerusalem to Rome in 30 years, and the writings of the Christian historian Eusebius of Caesarea, friend and admirer of the emperor Constantine, there is a period of over 200 years (AD 60–300) with little formal writing of history but considerable development. Persecution and martyrdom became increasingly a sign of the strength of Christianity as a movement, which aroused the fears of the authorities of the Roman empire. The letters of the early bishop of Antioch, Ignatius (c. 35–c. 107), on his way to martyrdom in Rome, have survived. They show that like many Christians of the early period he appeared to welcome his destiny.

The aged bishop of Smyrna (today's Izmir), Polycarp, who had heard the apostle John preach in his youth, was invited to abjure Christ to save his life. He replied,

'Eighty-six years have I served him and he has never done me wrong: how can I blaspheme my King and Saviour?' He was burned to death, probably in AD 155. A correspondence between the governor of Pontus in Asia Minor, Pliny the younger, and the emperor Trajan, written around AD 112, has survived, showing some attempt at leniency but also willingness to execute any intransigent Christians.

Emperors after Trajan, such as Decius (emperor 249–51) and Diocletian (emperor 284–305) instituted severe persecutions. There were sufficient Christians in North Africa for memorable martyrdoms to take place in Carthage of a young married woman called Perpetua and her slave girl Felicity, who were thrown to wild beasts after trial. It was also in North Africa that great problems were to be raised for church leaders by those who sought certificates (*libelli*) from the Roman authorities in time of

Modern icon of Perpetua and Felicity in the arena at Carthage.

persecution and then wished to reunite with the church. Cyprian, a great bishop of Carthage, grappled with this problem between 248 and 258. It was the North African, Tertullian (c. 160–c. 225), with his arresting style, who wrote that 'the blood of Christians is seed', often misquoted as 'the blood of the martyrs is the seed of the church'.

As well as North African Carthage, Egypt had become an important centre of Christianity. Alexandria, one of the great cities and centres of civilization in the ancient world, became also a centre of Christian learning. Three leading theologians and apologists (advocates) for the faith were connected with the school of theology there: Pantaenus, who died around 190 and who will appear in the next chapter as an early missionary to Asia, Clement of Alexandria (c. 150–215), and one of the great speculative minds of Christian history, Origen (c. 185–254). The ancient Egyptian church, the Coptic church, has existed until today, and it was Egypt that provided the seeds of monasticism, a movement of great importance for the church of the future, through pioneering ascetic saints such as Antony (c. 251–356) and Pachomios (c. 290–346). The latter emphasized community for monks. Egypt also produced one of the most influential Christians of all time in Athanasius (c. 296–373), bishop of Alexandria from 328, to whom we shall return.

Christian writings

The spread of Christianity also involved Christian writings. Paul's letters, written between AD 45 and AD 65 were addressed to Christian communities for the most part and to their problems of belief and behaviour. The Gospels, however, were aimed at persuading the unconvinced also. It is thought that Mark's was the first Gospel, probably dating AD 64, and by AD 100 the others were in circulation. As a form of literature they were unlike any other in the ancient world. They were not biographies or 'lives of Jesus', nor philosophical writings, nor histories. Perhaps the best description of them can be found in John: 'these are written so that you may come to believe that Jesus is the Christ, the Son of God, and that through believing you may have life in his name'(John 20:31). In our terms they might be thought of as extended tracts, inviting belief in Christ as the life-giver. Luke expressed his purpose to his unknown enquirer, Theophilus, as 'to write an orderly account for you, most excellent Theophilus, so that you may know the truth concerning the things about which you have been instructed' (Luke 1:3–4).

Christian literature did not, however, end with the epistles (letters) and Gospels, though with the formation of what became known as the canon (or list) of scriptural books they had a special status and recognition by the church from around 350. Apart from the earliest apostolic circle of writers, others set about advocating, defending

'Those who lived with reason, even though they were thought atheists, are Christians, as amongst the Greeks, Socrates and Heraclitus and men like them.'

JUSTIN, *APOLOGY*, I.46

and propagating Christianity. Justin (c. 100–c. 165), a teacher and philosopher who was born in Samaria, wrote his first and second *Apology* (c. 155; c. 161), and also his *Dialogue with Trypho*, which aimed at convincing Jews. He was martyred in Rome around 165.

Of the other 2nd-century 'apologists' as they were called, the best known to subsequent generations was the North African, Tertullian (c. 160–c. 225), already mentioned, a brilliant polemical writer from Carthage. Third-century Alexandria produced a sustained attempt to bring together Christianity and Hellenistic (Greek-based) civilization, and two successive thinkers at the head of the Alexandrian school of theology, Clement of Alexandria and Origen, already mentioned above, sought to answer the arguments of the pagan philosophers such as Celsus. Origen's reply, *Contra Celsum*, was written around 250.

In answering the question as to how Christianity made such headway against an all-powerful state like the Roman empire, so that the tide turned in the early years of the 4th century, the great German historian of the church, Adolf von Harnack, listed a number of cumulative causes of significance: the care of the sick, of widows; the Christians' attitude to death, whether through burial clubs or the respect they showed through their belief in resurrection both in general and when faced with martyrdom in the arena; their provision of support networks for the poor, the disadvantaged, even slaves all made an impact on a society where such things were rare and unusual. He quoted Tertullian's epigram, so often turned cynically on Christians since but highly significant when first used: 'See how these Christians love one another', indicating the social nature of the faith. The churches provided a kind of informal employment bureau for the needy, as well as being sources of hospitality.

Alexamenos Prays to His God. Graffito in a guardroom of the Emperor's palace on the Palatine in Rome, 2nd century AD.

'Constantine now turned to his father's God in prayer... it would be hard to believe if the emperor himself had not told me... and... swore that this was true. He saw a cross of light in the sky and the words "in this sign conquer"... I have myself seen the copy which the goldsmiths made for the emperor the next morning.'

EUSEBIUS, *LIFE OF CONSTANTINE*, 27–28

The ferocity of the persecution by emperors such as Decius and Diocletian gave evidence of the church as a strong alternative social association, which seemed to the emperors to be undermining the unity of the empire. Unlike the Jews, the Christians did not earn the right to be regarded as a *religio licita* (permitted religion); but they had a recognized social presence in the empire, to which even the graffiti in Rome of a crucified ass and its worshipper 'Alexamenos' who 'adores God' bore witness. Tertullian was still meeting this 2nd-century caricature in his *Apology*: 'You imagine the head of an ass to be our God.'

Roman approval

Constantine (c. 280–337), declared emperor in York in 306, transformed the situation of the church and its expansion. His great admirer, Eusebius of Caesarea, historian of the church and author of the *Ecclesiastical History* and the

Head from colossal statue of Constantine I, Rome.

Life of Constantine, to whom we owe much of our knowledge of the period, saw him as the divinely appointed deliverer and Christian leader, though Constantine was not baptized until near death. Before the decisive battle of Milvian Bridge in 312, as described by the Christian writer Lactantius (c. 250–325), he dreamed of the cross, in a special form known as the 'Labarum', which became his standard. After his victory he issued an edict of toleration in 313, the Edict of Milan, from which Christians benefited. He did his best to bring unity to the church, both where it faced schism in North Africa and over protracted divisions over doctrine.

One interesting aside on the extent to which Christianity had penetrated to the furthest reaches of the empire is that, when Constantine referred such issues to the Council of Arles in 314, we know that three British bishops attended, indicating a developed church life in Roman Britain.

Constantine's greatest attempt at uniting the church doctrinally was the Council of Nicea of 325, which was to have lasting effects. Here the Arian heresy, which had the effect of turning Christ into a demigod, was repudiated. Jesus was judged to be not only of similar 'substance' to God but identical (Greek: *homoousios* meaning of the same substance). It was a triumph for the upholders of orthodoxy, among them Athanasius, although Athanasius's immediate reward was to be exiled by Constantine to avoid further disputes.

Encouraged by imperial protection and approval, people flocked to join the churches, whatever problems of nominal Christianity they brought with them.

'Many people are joining the church in the city which is called by my name. The number of churches must be increased. I ask you to order fifty copies of the Holy Scriptures... as quickly as may be.'

CONSTANTINE TO EUSEBIUS, *LIFE OF CONSTANTINE*, 36

Pressures on the Roman
empire from about 370 to 470

Boundary of Roman Empire

Huns

Vandals

Visigoths

Ostrogoths

Jutes/Angles/Saxons

Franks

OSTROGOTHS

HUNS

VANDALS

VISIGOTHS

ACEDONIA

Philippi

Thessalonica

Constantinople

PONTUS

ARMENIA

Nicaea

CAPPADOCIA

Smyrna

Ephesus

Athens

Iconium

Lystra

Tarsus

Edessa

Nisibis

PERSIA

CRETE

CYPRUS

Antioch

Dura-Europos

Ctesiphon

SYRIA

Damascus

Samaria

Jerusalem

ARABIA

Alexandria

EGYPT

Roman decline

After Constantine's death in 337, the Roman empire
came under increasing pressure on its frontiers. Great
movements of peoples, notably the Huns from the steppes
of central Asia, pressed on other warrior groups such as
the Goths, who had already been opponents of the Roman
legions defending the empire's eastern boundaries. One
section of the Goths pressed down into the Balkans in the
370s, into Greece and up the shore of the Adriatic in the
390s. It was these Visigoths, as they were called, who
ultimately sacked the city of Rome itself, under their leader
Alaric in 410, a leader influenced by Arian Christianity.

Other pagan peoples such as the Franks, the Alans,
the Vandals and the Ostrogoths were also forcing their
way into the empire. The Vandals, who originated in the
steppes like the Huns, crossed the Rhine, moved into
Spain and across the straits of Gibraltar into North Africa.
Here they confronted a church made famous by Tertullian
and the great bishop of Carthage, Cyprian, martyred in
258 after heroic attempts to restore the unity of the
church, whose successor in terms of Christian stature was

Monica (c. 331–87)

Augustine's mother was probably herself a native of Thagaste near Hippo. She
married Patricius, a pagan, who was a potentially violent and frequently angry
husband. Nevertheless, Monica appears to have been responsible for him
becoming a Christian. He died when Augustine was 15, and Augustine refers to
him hardly at all in *The Confessions*. Monica was a Christian of strong convictions,
with a love of Augustine that was possessive but deep. She was widowed at 40,
but she was prepared to deny Augustine his home when he embraced the heresy
of Manichaeanism. She was ambitious for his success and followed him to Milan;
here she even questioned the great Ambrose on the church's failure to fast in the
way she approved. She was a strong influence towards Augustine's conversion, an
admirer of Ambrose and an ally in his effect on her son. When Augustine decided
to return to Africa from Italy after her prayers had been answered and he was
baptized, she died at Ostia in Italy in the same year.

Augustine, bishop of Hippo (354–430). Augustine, like Tertullian a brilliant writer and rhetorician, was born in Thagaste in modern Algeria, to a pagan father but a devoutly Christian mother, Monica. In his great work of autobiography *The Confessions* he recorded how, after a time of prolonged inner turmoil, he surrendered his life to Christ in a garden in Milan in 386, after hearing a child's voice repeating again and again '*tolle, lege*' ('take and read'), which prompted him to open Paul's epistles at the verses that proved decisive for him.

Augustine was finally baptized by Ambrose, bishop of Milan, whose preaching had greatly impressed him, in 387. Augustine became one of the greatest theologians of his or any age. In addition to *The Confessions* and *On the Trinity* he wrote a further great work *The City of God* between 413 and 426, in which he held the old pagan gods responsible for the sack of Rome by Alaric in 410. He reviewed the fortunes of secular empires like Rome but distinguished this from the image of the 'heavenly city', the city of God, only to be realized in the next life. His doctrine of the two cities became a leading influence in European thought in succeeding centuries. After Rome's fall, he could not but be aware of the 'barbarians at the gates', as the Vandals swept into North Africa and established a pagan kingdom, which included his town of Hippo, and, after his death, overcame Carthage in 439. This invasion of Latin North Africa, of which Tertullian, Cyprian and Augustine were towering figures, paved the way for the elimination of the Christian church by Muslim invasion, after Mohammed's death in 632.

CHAPTER 2

Asia to 1500

Thomas, the apostle of Christ, is linked by tradition to the spread of Christianity to the East. The Christian scholar and translator of the Bible, Jerome (c. 345–450), wrote in a letter: 'He [Jesus] was present in all places with Thomas in India, with Peter in Rome, with Paul in Illyria, with Titus in Crete, with Andrew in Greece, with each apostle and apostolic man in his own separate region' (*Letter to Marcellus*, 59). Eusebius of Caesarea, to whom, as we have seen, we owe much of our information on the period between Luke's writings and the time of Constantine (70–300), also connected Thomas with the spread north-east to the buffer kingdom of Osrhoene. Much of the early tradition about this kingdom and its capital, Edessa, and its reception of Christianity, is legendary, although there is no doubt that Edessa became an extremely important centre of Christian vitality later.

Coin of Abgar VIII of Edessa.

According to Eusebius, Thomas received a request from Abgar, king of Edessa, for healing and responded by sending Thaddaeus, one of the 72 disciples mentioned in Luke 10, to the king. Eusebius also included in his history the legend of a letter from Abgar to Jesus himself, again requesting healing, but this letter and Jesus' reply are spurious.

Nevertheless, geographically Edessa was on the old silk road north from Antioch, such an important early centre of Christian life, and there is a tradition of martyrdoms in Edessa contemporary with Pliny's persecution on the borders of the empire in 112. It is thought that Abgar VIII may have become a

Christian in 177. We know of a very early Christian church, destroyed in Edessa in 201, the oldest Christian public building beyond the borders of the Roman empire yet known.

Adiabene and Armenia

Before pursuing the tradition of Thomas's travels in India, two other kingdoms deserve mention, both centres of Christian life in early days. Osrhoene (and Edessa) was a 'client kingdom', a buffer between two mighty empires, Rome to the west and Persia to the east. The Parthians, who ruled in Persia, also maintained the kingdom of Adiabene, with its capital Arbela, further east than Edessa and north of the River Tigris. Here again there is a tradition of Christian martyrdoms between AD 117 and AD 123. Uncertain tradition has linked Christianity in Adiabene to Osrhoene – a disciple of Thaddaeus (or Addai) was said to have reached the kingdom and, according to a 6th-century document, even appointed a bishop called Pkidha in 104.

With the kingdom of Armenia, however, there is more solid historical ground. It lay north of Edessa in the mountainous area between the Black Sea and the Caspian. It has the historical distinction of being the first state to embrace Christianity as a national religion, pre-dating the conversion of Constantine and his imperial victory of 312. The missionary to Armenia was Gregory the Illuminator (c. 240–332). He may have been a member of the royal family of Armenia but had grown up in exile in Cappadocia, possibly because his father had been involved in the assassination of the king. He returned to Armenia and, through his witness, King Tiridates (c. 238–314) became a Christian, so possibly converted by the son of his father's assassin. Gregory's son succeeded him as bishop and is known to have attended the Council of Nicea in 325. Armenian Christianity has remained a distinctive and important brand of the faith, with some 5 million professing allegiance to the Armenian church today.

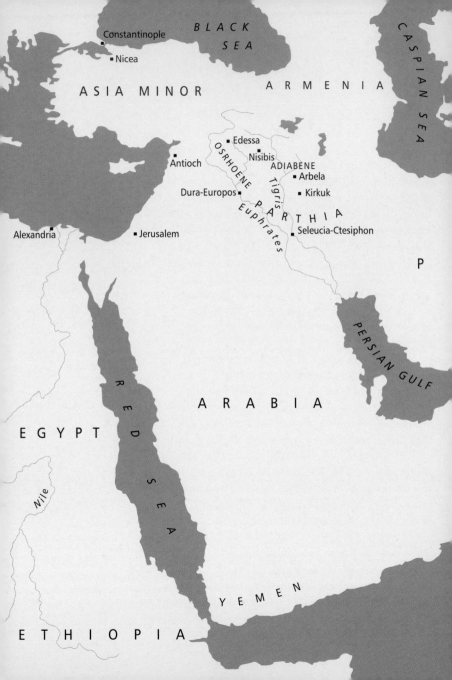

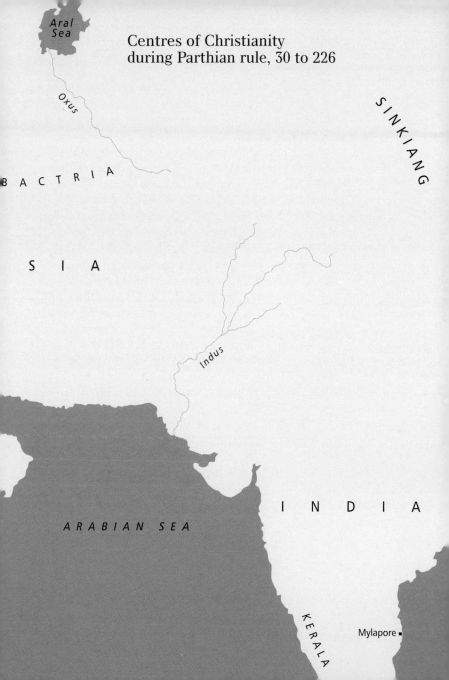

Centres of Christianity
during Parthian rule, 30 to 226

Aral
Sea

Oxus

SINKIANG

BACTRIA

SIA

Indus

ARABIAN SEA

INDIA

KERALA

Mylapore ▪

*'He [Pantaenus]
preached Christ
to the Brahmans
and philosophers
of India.'*

JEROME, C. 400

India

The traditions linking Thomas to India are more than
Jerome's letter but they remain a source of dispute. There
are still so-called 'Thomas Christians' in South India today,
who use a Syriac form of worship (Syriac being a branch of
Aramaic, probably the language spoken by Jesus himself,
used in Edessa and its surroundings) and based as a very
ancient Christian community in south-west India in
Kerala. There is a tomb and shrine in honour of Thomas
at Mylapore, built of bricks used by a Roman trading
colony but not in use after AD 50. A song, written down in
1601 but passed on in Kerala for 50 generations, would
also place Thomas around this date. It is known that many
trading vessels crossed to India in the 1st century, when
the secret of the monsoon winds was discovered, a
discovery that led to over 100 such trading vessels a year
crossing from the Red Sea to India. Seventh and 8th-
century crosses have been found and the
shrine of Mylapore was revered and seen
by Marco Polo (c. 1254–1324).

Carving of
St Thomas from
Mylapore tomb,
Madras, India.

Alongside the southern tradition,
Thomas has also been connected to the
north of India and to King Gundaphur.
An inscription discovered in 1890 and
coins suggest a 20-year reign from
AD 19, giving external confirmation to
the somewhat discredited document,
the *Acts of Thomas*, written in Edessa,
with its reference to the 'Great King
Gundaphora', in whose kingdom in North
India Thomas was said to have worked.
It is not impossible, but historically
unproven, that Thomas visited North
India but died in South India, where by
tradition he was martyred. One hundred
years later, according to Jerome,
Pantaenus, the head of a great school of
theology in Alexandria before Clement

and Origen, left Alexandria to 'preach Christ to the Brahmans' of India, a development recorded by Eusebius. He wrote of Pantaenus in the *Ecclesiastical History* that he was 'a herald of the gospel of Christ to the nations of the East... sent as far as India'. India may have been evangelized by an apostle and visited by a famous Alexandrian theologian by the year AD 200.

Persia and the church of the East
The Persian empire, as much as the Roman empire, was the scene of expanding Christianity in the first three centuries, as it was also the source of persecutions of even greater severity than those of imperial Rome before Constantine. The Parthian dynasty, which had used Osrhoene and Adiabene as client kingdoms, gave way to the Sassanids after AD 226. By then, Christians had not only reached Persia but the steppes of Asia, and even Bactria, an area of northern Afghanistan today – this according to the Christian scholar, Bardaisan, writing around 196 in Edessa, where he wrote of Christian 'sisters among the Gilaurians and Bactrians'. An inscription, discovered by W.M. Ramsey in 1883, appears to point to a bishop from Asia Minor who met Bardaisan of Edessa and also found Christians beyond the River Euphrates with whom he shared the eucharist; the inscription could date as early as 150–200.

Nisibis was to replace Edessa as the great theological centre of the East; but the capital of the Sassanid empire, Seleucia-Ctesiphon, south of modern Baghdad, became the centre of church authority. On the disputed border of the two empires the victorious Persians overcame the fortress town of Dura-Europos in AD 250 near to the River Euphrates. This site has since revealed a very early Christian church, transformed from a private house into a full scale church around AD 230–50, with a baptistery and wall paintings of Christ the Good Shepherd and a mural of the women at the tomb of the resurrection. A hundred years later Eusebius the historian met a bishop at the

'He [Pantaenus] was a most learned man... he taught at the Christian college at Alexandria... sent as far as the land of the Indians. He found the people there who knew of Christ and already had St Matthew's Gospel.'

EUSEBIUS,
ECCLESIASTICAL HISTORY, 10.1–3

'Christ has planted the new race of Christians in every nation.'

BARDAISAN,
CHRISTIAN NOBLEMAN AND SCHOLAR OF EDESSA,
C. 190

*'There were
bishops in other
cities, too.
Nisibis and
Ctesiphon did
not yet have
bishops because
of fear of the
pagans.'*

CHRONICLE OF
ARBELA

*'God added
to their
[missionary
monks'] years
for the sake of
religion. He used
them to lead
nearly all the
Syrian nation
and many
Persians to the
true faith.'*

SOZOMEN ON EARLY
MONASTIC
MISSIONARIES

Council of Nicea in 325 whom he described as 'bishop of
the whole of Persia and in the great India'. There is other
evidence for a missionary bishop, David, around 300 in
Basra at the head of the Persian Gulf. By the early 300s,
bishops of Seleucia-Ctesiphon had national authority in
Persia.

Whereas the Parthian rulers of Persia had been
religiously tolerant, there was a change of front after
Constantine under the Sassanids. The Persian empire
had been a place of refuge for Christians from Roman
persecution, although Zoroastrianism remained the
religion of Persia. While Rome was the enemy of both
Persian and Christian alike all would be well. Now,
however, Constantine made no secret of
his links with Christians in the Persian
empire, which made Christians a
potential fifth column as viewed by
Persian rulers. One Christian theologian
was unwise enough to prophesy Persian
defeat by Rome. After 340 persecution of
bitter ferocity was fuelled by the enmity
of Zoroastrians. On Good Friday 344, 100
Christian priests were beheaded in front
of their bishop, Simon, and then he and
other bishops were executed. The
historian of the times, Sozomen, who
tried to provide a sequel to Eusebius's
history by covering the period 323–425,
wrote of many thousands of Christians
being martyred up to a possible total of
190,000. The worst persecution seems to
have lasted for 40 years (339–79) until
the death of Sharpur II. Although more
severe than that of the Roman
emperors, accounts of apostasy by
Christians of the East are few by
comparison. Further periods of
persecution followed, less long but no

less severe, in 419–20, 420–22, 445–48. In one case alone, at Kirkuk in northern Mesopotamia, 10 bishops and 153,000 others were massacred.

Theological division

In a century in which Alaric the Goth sacked Rome in 410, a highly significant date for the church of the East was that of the Council of Chalcedon in 451. We have seen earlier that debate about the deity of Christ had been central to the Council of Nicea in 325, when he was declared to be of the same substance as the Father and Arianism was denounced. At Chalcedon the debate centred on the two natures of Christ, divine and human, and it was

The Armenian church of St Thaddeus, known locally as Ghara Kilissa (Black Church). Near Maku, eastern Azerbaijan province, Iran.

*'To put it
pictorially, the
Monophysites
followed the
tradition of
"wine and
water" – that in
the incarnate
Lord the divine
and the human
merged into
one... the
Nestorians that
of "oil and
water" – in Jesus
the divine and
human
remained
distinct.'*

STEPHEN NEILL,
CHRISTIAN MISSIONS

highly significant for the church of the East because the position it held was judged to be unorthodox.

The debate was sophisticated and complex but the loser in it was the Christian leader Nestorius, patriarch of Constantinople. Broadly, those who emphasized the unity of the two natures (*monophysite*: single nature) regarded Nestorius as in error for emphasizing the two natures too heavily, to the point of separation. It is by no means certain that this is what Nestorius taught but in so far as the church of the East took a Nestorian position it was regarded by those in the West to be heretical. Many writings will still refer to the Christians of the East as 'Nestorians'.

By the year 500 there were effectively three main branches of the Christian church: the church of the West, which looked to Rome and Constantinople; the church of Africa, with its great centre in Alexandria and with the church in Ethiopia; and the church of the East, with its centre in Persia and its great missionary school of theology transferred from Edessa to Nisibis around 471 led by the famous theologian Narsai, who died in 503. At its largest this school had 1,000 students. The church of the East mounted successful missions among nomad peoples after 450 and spread Christianity across central Asia between 450 and 650. These included missions among the Huns, west of the Caspian Sea, conducted by Nestorian bishops and priests. Another missionary leader, Abraham of Kaskar (491–586), revived the monastic communities of the church and provided further spiritual vitality.

In addition to suffering schism from the West, the church of the East now had to endure the invasion of the Persian empire. Arabia had not been without Christian influence and there had been a bishop from Qatar present at the Council of Nicea in 325. There had also been a Christian ruler. Queen Mawwiyya, whose forces defeated those of Emperor Valens after her husband's death in 373, had insisted on receiving an orthodox bishop before she would make peace. There were Christian missions in the south-east of Arabia in Yemen: before the birth of Mohammed in 570 both Nestorian and monophysite missions had established themselves around 500.

The development of Islam in the next century was to have far-reaching effects in Persia and on its capital, Seleucia-Ctesiphon, which fell to the Arabs in 637, as on the church of the East as a whole. Muslim authorities could be tolerant of religious minorities but, as communities known as *dhimmi*, they often became religious ghettoes sapped of their vitality. Nevertheless, contemporary with the Muslim invasions, the church of the East had made its greatest leap forward, with its missionaries entering China at the same time as Aidan was taking the mission from Iona to Northumbria in Britain in 635.

China: the first entry

There have been few more dramatic archaeological finds or inscriptions than the stone of Hsianfu in China. This was a black limestone monument just under nine feet (three metres) tall, which was discovered by Chinese workmen in 1623 when digging. It told of Christian mission in the person of one Alopen, who was in the capital of the T'ang dynasty in 635. Up to its discovery, the earliest-known Christian presence in China of missionaries was that of the Franciscans from 1245. The monument had been erected in 781. It commemorated the arrival of 'the Te-chin (Syrian) illustrious religion' in China and was written in Chinese characters under the symbol of a cross emerging from a lotus blossom. It advanced Western knowledge of Christianity in China by hundreds of years. Nestorian Christians may have been in China as early as 450 and there is evidence of a Persian missionary in China outside the Great Wall at Wei in 455: but the mission of Alopen received imperial favour from an emperor of the T'ang dynasty.

T'ai-tsung (emperor 627–49) owned a library

'Having carefully examined the scope of his [Alopen's] teaching we find it mysteriously spiritual and of silent operation... this teaching is helpful to all creatures and beneficial to all men. So let it have free course throughout the empire.'

EDICT OF
TOLERATION OF 638
IN CHINA

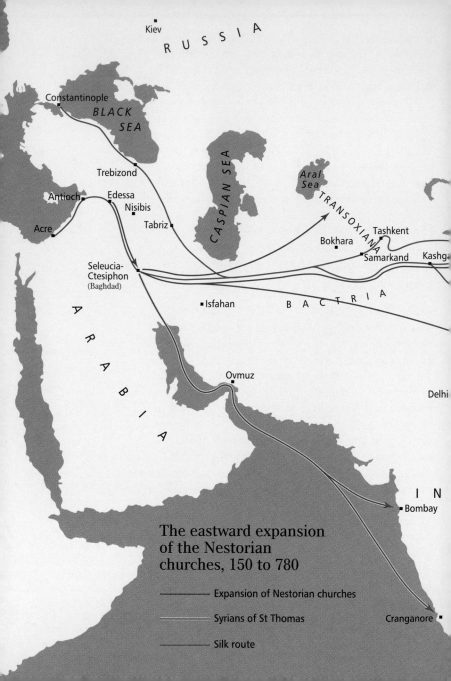

The eastward expansion
of the Nestorian
churches, 150 to 780

——— Expansion of Nestorian churches

——— Syrians of St Thomas

——— Silk route

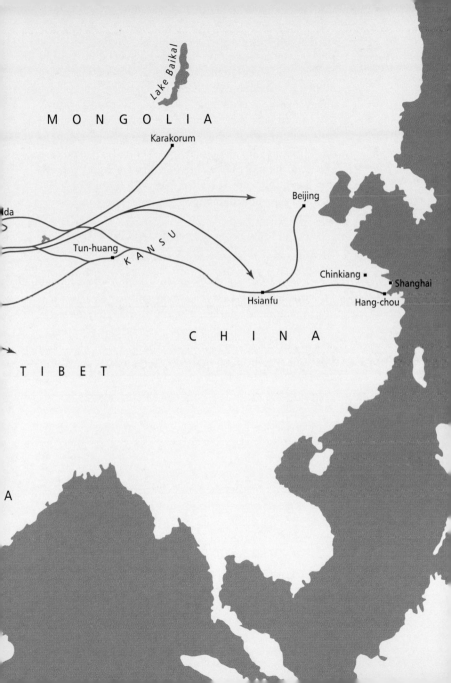

comparable to the great library of Alexandria, with some 200,000 volumes; he may have had a special interest in the addition of Christian literature to this collection. He set Alopen to translate the Christian scriptures and published an edict of toleration in 638, which is recorded on the monument. His capital had Buddhist and Taoist temples built with imperial funds – support he also extended to the Christians for the building of a church. The edict also told of 21 monks in China in 638, probably all Persian. It is likely that they travelled over 4,000 miles (6,400 kilometres) from their church's main centre in Seleucia-Ctesiphon.

By the time the tablet was erected in 781 the

'The Persian scriptural religion began in Syria. By preaching and practice it came and long ago spread to China... it is necessary to get back to the original name. Its Persian monasteries shall therefore be changed to Syrian monasteries throughout the empire.'

CHINESE EDICT OF
AD 754

Inscriptions from the stone of Hsianfu

There was in Persia a Lofty Virtue [i.e. a bishop] named A-lo-pen... he brought the true scriptures... rode through hardship and danger and in the ninth year of Cheng-Kuan [AD 635] arrived at Ch'ang-an... the Emperor received him as guest in the palace... the scriptures were translated in the library.

One Person of our Three-One became incarnate, the illustrious honoured one, Messiah, hid away his true majesty and came into the world as a man. An angel proclaimed the joy. A virgin bore a Sage in Syria. A bright star was the propitious portent, Persians saw its glory and came to offer gifts.

He hung, a brilliant sun, which scattered the regions of darkness. The devil's guile, lo, he was utterly cut off. He rowed mercy's barge, to go up to the course of light. The souls of men, lo, he has already saved. His mighty task once done, at noonday he ascended into heaven.

TEXT OF HSIANFU MONUMENT OF 781

Christian church had made considerable advances, especially between 712 and 781. An example of this was the Christian leader called Issu, who had caused the stone to be put in place, and was both a general in the Chinese army and also a Nestorian Christian priest. One sign of China's awareness of political realities in the west of Asia was an edict to show that Christianity went behind a Muslim dominated Persia to origins in 'Syria'. So, in 754 all Christian monasteries previously known as Persian were to be known as Syrian.

After 781, however, and the fall of the T'ang dynasty,

Nestorian Stone (detail from top of stele).

the Nestorian church in China vanished, perhaps through overdependence on the T'ang rulers. There is a record of a Nestorian monk meeting an Arab called Abdul Faraj, who told him in 987 that Christianity was extinct in China. It was not to reappear until the days of the Great Khans and the Mongols and then through Franciscan missionaries. Meanwhile, between 500 and 1000, Nestorian Christianity, if weakened in China, had shown an extraordinary resilience in central Asia, so that the seven metropolitan areas based on Adiabene, Nisibis and other centres, became 15 by AD 1000 and included areas such as Turkestan and Samarkand by 781, India by 800 as well as outreach around the Caspian Sea and to the north. All this meant a strengthened church organization, despite the influence of Zoroastrianism and Islam in the Persian empire.

China during the Mongols

Among the tribal groups reached by Nestorian missionaries in central Asia were a people known as Keraits, who had settled near Lake Baikal. Some 200,000 of these people including a Kerait prince sought baptism, according to a letter to John VI, the Nestorian patriarch in Baghdad, in 1009. Nearly 200 years later, a tribal chief and Christian leader of this people became patron of a young man who was the son of a chief of a subordinate clan. This young man, known as Temujin, became in due course Genghis (Chinghis) Khan (1162–1227). He was never a Christian but, like other Mongol rulers, he was not opposed to Christianity. He moved first to the east in conquest towards Pekin (Beijing) but then to the west in overrunning Transoxiana, northern Iran and Persia. He destroyed Bokhara and Samarkand, defeated the Georgians in 1221 and the forces of southern Russia in 1223.

Although he died in 1227, his son returned to the west and invaded Russia in 1236, took Kiev and invaded northern Poland, Hungary and Austria; a raiding party even reached Albania. Genghis Khan himself was buried with traditional Mongol 'shamanistic' ceremony, which included the sacrifices of 50 young women and equivalent numbers of horses towards the next life. His successors remained tolerant of Christians and Kublai Khan (1215–94), whose territorial dominions stretched from the Pacific to Constantinople and who ruled both China and Persia, was to welcome Franciscan missionaries from the West.

Pope Innocent IV (Pope 1243–54), confronted by Mongol presence in Europe, sent the first emissary and missionary to the Mongol court in 1245. He was a Franciscan, who had known the founder of the order and

Portrait of Genghis Khan.

'In Xanadu did Kubla Khan a stately pleasure-dome decree, where Alph the sacred river ran, through caverns measureless to man, down to a sunless sea. So twice five miles of fertile ground with walls and towers were girdled round and there were gardens bright with sinuous rills, where blossom'd many an incense-bearing tree.'

S.T. COLERIDGE,
KUBLA KHAN

was called John of Plano Carpini. After this there were more approaches by western Christians to the Mongol court, which were as much political as missionary in a religious sense, made up of Franciscan and Dominican friars. William of Rubruck, who visited between 1253 and 1255, left accounts of the Mongols and of religious debate before the Great Khan, in which Muslims, Nestorian Christians, Zoroastrians and his own brand of western Catholicism took part. William had a personal conversation with Mongke, grandson of Genghis Khan and Great Khan from 1251–59, who displayed characteristic Mongol openness to the friar but left him in no doubt that traditional Mongol shamanism was his own choice.

In addition to the Franciscan missionaries, the

William of Rubruck (c. 1215–c. 1260)

William came from Rubruck (Rubroek), a Flemish-speaking village in northern France. He joined the Franciscan order, and he became acquainted with Louis IX of France, the devout king later to become St Louis. His visit to the Mongol court was made with the king's blessing, after Louis had heard that a Mongol prince had become a Christian. William travelled from Acre in 1252 and reported to the king on what he found at the Mongol court in his *Itinerary of Friar William*. As a Franciscan western Catholic, he was severely critical of what he found of Christianity in China, whether among the Uighurs and other tribal groups, or at the court, where he did, however, recognize a better-grounded Nestorian Christianity. In his view, perhaps biased, the Nestorian priests engaged in magic themselves and failed to condemn it in others; and indulged in raucous drunkenness, while Nestorian Christians were pictured as polygamous, corrupt, untrustworthy and given to usury. He returned to Acre in 1255 and later visited Paris, where he shared his knowledge with the Englishman Roger Bacon in 1257.

famous Italian merchants and travellers the brothers Polo, father and uncles of Marco, reached the court of Kublai Khan in 1266. Kublai Khan welcomed the brothers and showed great interest in their religion. He sent a letter to the pope that requested 100 missionaries.

The pope's response was to send two Dominican friars with the Polos (Marco accompanied his uncles on this journey) in 1275 but the Dominicans turned back. This was an opportunity lost, as the Great Khan had shown sympathy, but after 1280 his power began to wane. By the time the fresh missionaries arrived from Rome in 1294 the last of the great Mongol Khans had died in that year. According to Marco Polo's accounts, after spending some 16 years in China, he estimated some 700,000 Christians were in the region that he knew and it is possible that some of these were survivors from earlier Nestorian missions, commemorated by the monument of 781. He reported on three beautiful churches in Kamsu province and Christian churches in another 11 cities. Independently of Marco Polo, it is known that there was a Christian community of 2,000 in Chinkiang, a city of hundreds of thousands, where the Yangtse and the Grand Canal intersected.

Marco Polo told of a Christian prince, George, who was the issue of one of Genghis Khan's daughters and a Christian father, who first married Kublai Khan's granddaughter and then, after her death, married the daughter of Timur (Timur Lang) (1336–1405). This is the ravager of China, the man known to history as Tamerlane, following the English playwright Christopher Marlowe. Under the influence of the Franciscans, George the prince became a follower of western Christianity and built the first Roman Catholic place of worship in China when king of the Ongut tribe. He died later in battle, leading one of Timur's armies.

The Franciscan missionaries, notably John of Montecorvino (1246–1330), who had been himself a soldier, a doctor in the service of the emperor Frederick II

'You shall go to your High Priest [the pope] and shall pray him to send me a hundred men skilled in your religion... so I shall be baptized and then all my barons and great men and then their subjects.'

THE POLOS

in Europe and finally a friar, claimed to have 6,000 converts in China by 1305. Pope Clement V created him archbishop of Peking in 1307. He was reinforced by three more bishops around 1313 in a party of seven missionaries sent to help him, some of whom were martyred by Muslims en route near Bombay. Another Franciscan, Odoric of Pordenone (c. 1265–1331), who wrote a popular account of his visit to China for European consumption, may have been the source of an estimate of 30,000 Christians in China.

The 12th century is considered the period when Nestorian Christianity spread most widely in Asia during the so-called *pax Mongolica* (Mongol era of peace). It was a time when the Mongol patriarch Mark (Maryaballah III)

Kublai Khan hands a message for the pope to the Polos. Illumination from *Le Livre de Merveilles du Monde*.

had a wider authority than the pope himself from his centre in Baghdad. His friend and associate, the Nestorian bishop Samma, visited Rome, Paris and Edward I's court in French Gascony; and was invited to celebrate mass according to the Eastern rite in Rome by Pope Nicholas IV on a visit in 1287–88.

Before the end of the Khans, one reign of savagery remained. Timur the Great (Tamerlane) has been judged to have possessed even greater ferocity than Genghis Khan but with none of his statesmanship. He conquered Persia in 1379 after 10 years as ruler of Samarkand; he sacked Delhi, killing Muslims and Christians indiscriminately; he incorporated Mesopotamia in his empire and defeated the Ottoman Turks in 1402 and the Egyptian Mamelukes. Unlike Genghis Khan he was no friend to Christians. His campaigns, coming on top of the withering of Christian communities under Muslim rule, meant that Nestorian Christianity was destroyed. The same went for those communities known as the Jacobites, who had emphasized the single nature of Christ. Only two enclaves of any strength remained, in the East: Malabar, where the 'Thomas Christians' remained and the centre of Cisre on the Upper Tigris. Timur had prepared the way for further Muslim advances, which led to the loss of the great cities of Jerusalem, Antioch and, finally, Constantinople, which fell to Muslim Turks in 1454.

The church of the East had

shown great vitality, never more so than in the Mongol period. Despite the benevolent neutrality of the Great Khans, however, it had never had a Constantine in the alternative empire of Persia, let alone in imperial China. The history of the Nestorian missions was still a very notable one, not least in reaching out with success to nomadic peoples such as the Keraits. It had many great achievements before the advent of the church of the West in the Franciscan and Dominican missions in China, themselves limited in their impact. Asian Christianity had a remarkable history from the early days in Antioch, Edessa and Nisibis (from, say, AD 40–500) right up to the Great Khans of 1150–1300. As this historical reflection switches to the modern period, launched by the voyages of Vasco da Gama to India of 1498 and followed by the advent of Jesuits and others in India, China and Japan, those great achievements over some 1300 years by Nestorian Christians over the vast distances of the Asian continent should be remembered.

CHAPTER 3

Europe to 1500

Turning from the East to mainland Europe, the spread of Christianity after Constantine's conversion can initially be viewed in the two corners of Europe. In the south-east corner, an influential mission was mounted among the Goths by Ulphilas (311–83). He was born in a country peopled by the Goths, Cappadocia, now part of northern Turkey. Although living in Constantinople as a young man, he absorbed the language and culture of this pagan people. He was made a bishop in Constantinople but he returned to his homeland as a missionary. Like so many missionaries, then and now, he became a translator of the scriptures. According to one Christian writer, he deliberately omitted the books of Kings, realizing that the Goths, a warlike people, needed no further encouragement to do battle. In theology he became Arian. As we have seen, the effect of Arius's teaching on Jesus was to turn him into a kind of demigod, a position ultimately repudiated by orthodoxy. The effect of Ulphilas's mission lasted for centuries but it included this Arian influence on the tribes of the Goths that he touched.

'They followed him... for he had faced danger for the faith, while many Goths were still heathen.'

SOZOMEN ON
ULPHILAS AND
THE GOTHS

Irish missionaries

In the extreme north-east of Europe, there was the romantic story of Patrick (c. 450). He had been brought up in the west country of Celto-British England, the son of a town councillor and Christian deacon, who was also a landowner and farmer. Aged 16, Patrick was kidnapped by Irish pirates and spent some years as a shepherd in Ireland. He escaped to Britain with, as he felt, divine assistance and decided to study for the Christian ministry. He returned to Ireland and

St Patrick.
Stained-glass
window in
Gloucester
Cathedral,
England.

*'I came to the
Irish peoples to
preach the
gospel and
endure the
taunts of
unbelievers...
losing my
birthright of
freedom for the
benefit of
others.'*

PATRICK,
CONFESSION

spent the rest of his life as an evangelist, Christian educator and promoter of communities of monks and nuns. In Trinity College, Dublin, there is a 1,000-year-old manuscript, copied from his own writing, it is claimed, giving the defence and account of his life, his *Confession*. The hymn known as St Patrick's Breastplate, which begins, 'I bind unto myself this day, the strong name of the Trinity', is thought to date some three centuries after his death.

Patrick was the first of a large number of saints and missionaries connected with Ireland. Perhaps the most considerable of these was Columba (c. 521–97), a prince of royal blood, who left Ireland in 563 to found the famous monastery on Iona. From this foothold off the Scottish coast, he worked among the North Picts as the British missionary, Ninian (? 390), according to Bede, worked among the South Picts, in the neighbourhood of Whithorn. Again according to Bede, Columba was responsible for the conversion of the king, and it was from Iona that Aidan (d. 651), another Irishman and monk, went to Northumbria in response to a request for help from

The 10th-century St Martin's Cross stands in front of the cathedral on Iona Island, Scotland. The cathedral dates from the 13th century.

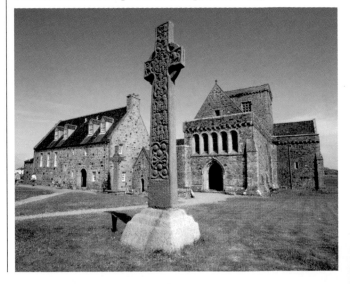

King Oswald (c. 605–42). The monks of Iona had been instrumental in Oswald's conversion when he was in exile in Scotland. Aidan became bishop of Lindisfarne, like Iona an island retreat but, unlike Iona, connected to the mainland at low tide. Aidan, we are told by Bede, through his holy life, gentleness and 'grace of discretion', won over the Northumbrians, despite being warned against them by a previous missionary as being intractable, harsh and barbarous in disposition. It is an interesting parallel that Aidan's mission to Northumbria was contemporary with that of Alopen in China noted in the last chapter.

Aidan was succeeded by another great figure, Cuthbert (c. 636–87), who became bishop of Lindisfarne in 685 and, after a period as a hermit on the Farne Islands, was buried at Lindisfarne two years later. As a sign of the ravages of the Viking raiders in the succeeding centuries, his body (a precious relic to northern Christians) was exhumed and found its ultimate resting place in Durham Cathedral. Here his tomb can be seen today, with other visible

'He never sought or cared for any worldly possessions and loved to give away to the poor.'

BEDE ON AIDAN

Bede (673–735)

Known to us as the Venerable Bede, he was the outstanding scholar of Anglo-Saxon England. He was put in the care of the monastery of Wearmouth and its abbot, Benedict Biscop, at the age of seven. When the new Benedictine monastery of Jarrow was founded in 682, Bede became a monk there for the rest of his life. He wrote on a variety of subjects but biblical commentaries and history were his main works. Among the first, he wrote expositions of the Gospels of Mark and Luke and the Acts of the Apostles. He is most widely remembered today for his remarkable *Ecclesiastical History of the English Nation* (finished in 731), still our chief source of knowledge of its period, which justly earned him the title of the 'father of English history'. It bears comparison with Luke's Acts, with its striking word pictures of leading figures and its vivid set pieces. Like Luke, his careful accounts do not baulk at the miraculous. He wrote also the life of Cuthbert, both in verse and prose, and was responsible for creating a Europe-wide cult of the saint. Appropriately, the tombs of Cuthbert and Bede lie now at the east and west end of Durham Cathedral.

reminders of Celtic Christianity in Northumbria, a culture
that produced treasures such as the Lindisfarne Gospels
(c. 696). Like the Irish Book of Kells (c. 800), this
illuminated manuscript of great beauty somehow escaped
the depredations of these centuries. While Columba
and Aidan went to Scotland and Northumbria as Irish
missionaries, another Irish saint, Columbanus (d. 615),
left Ireland around 590 to spend the rest of his life in
peregrinatio (wandering pilgrimage) in modern France,
where he founded monastic communities in the Vosges
region of Gaul at Luxeuil and elsewhere, before ending
his days in a monastic house at Bobbio in northern Italy.

Evangelizing Europe's tribes
Mainland Europe was peopled by largely pagan tribes,
of whom the Franks later assumed great importance;
but Friesians in the Netherlands, Saxons further east,
Burgundians and Lombards in northern Italy all invited
evangelization. As well as the Irish pilgrim missionaries,
two highly significant Englishmen left their stamp on
the tribes of northern Europe, both also doing much to
enhance the authority of the popes in Rome on their
missions. Willibrord (658–739) was a Northumbrian
Christian, educated at Ripon, where he knew another
famous churchman, Wilfred. Willibrord became a
missionary to the Friesians. In 695 he was consecrated
as their archbishop by the pope and subsequently
founded a cathedral at Utrecht and a famous monastery
at Echternach in Luxembourg. He also carried out
missionary work in Denmark and elsewhere.

Boniface (c. 675–754) was probably born in Crediton
in Devon, then in the kingdom of Wessex. He helped
Willibrord in Friesia and carried out successful missions
to the Hessians further south. He was made a bishop in
Rome in 722 and earned undying fame by the symbolic act
of cutting down the Oak of Thor at Geissen. Thor was the
pagan god from whose name we still have our Thursday
('Thor's day'). This decisive and revolutionary action

caused many Hessians to acknowledge the superior power of the Christian religion. In 746 Boniface became archbishop of Mainz. He worked hard to re-establish the organization of the church east of the Rhine but after some years resigned in order to return to his missionary work. In Friesia, while awaiting a large confirmation at Dokkum in 754, he was set upon by a marauding party and

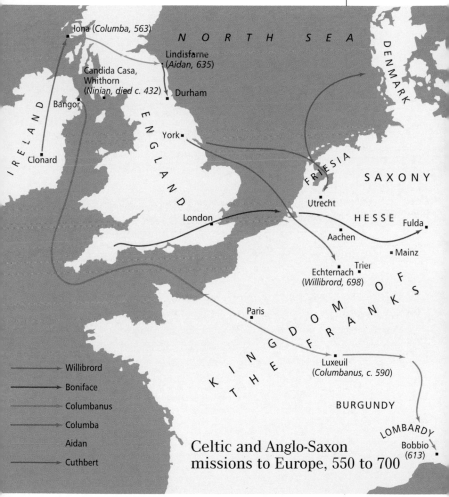

Celtic and Anglo-Saxon missions to Europe, 550 to 700

killed in his 80th year. The book he held up to protect his head from the sword, bloodstained and deeply cut, was a collection of the writings of Ambrose, bishop of Milan (d. 397) and mentor of Augustine of Hippo, which survives among other relics of this 'Apostle of Germany'. The English historian Christopher Dawson wrote of Boniface that he was 'a man who had deeper influence on the history of Europe than any Englishman who ever lived'.

The influence of the popes had already reached Britain. One of the greatest of all popes, Gregory I, 'the Great', loved to play on words. It is known that he made a pun of Angli (Angles, another northern people) as placed 'at the angle of the world'. It is by no means impossible that he also made the famous remark attributed to him on seeing fair-haired Anglo-Saxons in the slave market at Rome: '*Angli sunt, angeli fiant.*' ('They are Angles, they may become angels.') Legend or not, this missionary-minded pope dispatched a group of missionaries to Britain in 596 under another Augustine to the court of the kingdom of Kent, where a Christian princess had married a pagan king, Ethelbert (c. 560–616). Gregory showed great missionary acumen, advising that heathen places

Hilda of Whitby (614–80)

Leadership by Christian women was known early in the church's life. Hilda was a Northumbrian princess, who was among the many baptized by Paulinus in 627. When her sister became a nun in France, Hilda intended to join her, but Aidan wanted to secure her gifts for the English church. Through his influence, she became abbess of a monastery at Hartlepool, but in 657, she herself founded a religious house for men and women at Whitby, of which she became abbess. Here the famous synod of 664 was held. Hilda supported the Celtic side of the debate but, when the Roman way was adopted, she accepted the decision loyally. Bede wrote of her that her acquaintances called her mother because of her wonderful devotion and grace and as one who brought about the amendment of many from a distance 'who heard the inspiring story of her industry and goodness'.

of worship could be used for Christian services and pagan feasts and festivals incorporated into the Christian pattern.

In due course, as in so many tribal missions, Ethelbert as king and tribal chief was converted and baptized along with 10,000 of his subjects. Augustine became the first archbishop of Canterbury. Paulinus, a missionary monk who had joined the Roman mission, went north and baptized Edwin, king of Northumbria, and thousands of his subjects in 627, becoming bishop of York. Bede tells us that he did nothing but baptize for 36 days in a river near York, where the local centre for the worship of Woden (from which we derive our Wednesday) was set on fire and destroyed. Paulinus's baptisms prepared the way for Aidan's Celtic revival after 635 in Northumbria. The two traditions, Celtic and Roman, with their different customs, especially over the timing of Easter, met in conference at the Synod of Whitby in 664, when the Roman way on the celebration of the great festival and other things was accepted.

'The heathen temples of these people need not be destroyed, only the idols which are to be found in them.'

GREGORY THE GREAT

Charlemagne and Europe

It was not only the popes who were a growing authority in Europe. The Franks were developing into a dominant influence, whose political history was to be intertwined with the spiritual authority of the papacy. Charles Martel (c. 689–741) was strictly the mayor of the Frankish palace and court, but his prowess as a soldier and leader made him effectively ruler. Islam had penetrated into Spain and Muslim armies reached into southern Gaul. In a decisive battle, Martel (literally, the Hammer) defeated the Muslim forces at Tours in 732, pinning Muslim influence south of the Pyrenees and ending the prospect of an invasion of Gaul and northern Europe. Charles Martel sent his sons to be educated in the famous monastery of St Denis. One became a monk, but the other, Pepin, with the agreement of the pope, became king of the Franks not only by possession (like his father) but by right in 753. He repaid the church's support by helping the development of the

church put in hand by Willibrord and Boniface. His more famous son, Charlemagne, again allied himself with the pope and was crowned as emperor in Rome by Pope Leo III on Christmas Day 800.

Charlemagne's rule was strong but often ruthless. He was in favour of Christian learning and employed the scholarly Northumbrian theologian, Alcuin (c. 740–804), to foster learning at his court. Nevertheless, those Saxon tribes vanquished by the Frankish armies were often confronted with the choice of forcible baptism or death. Alcuin, to his credit, remonstrated against such practices, knowing that true faith cannot be imposed by force, but Charlemagne was determined to reduce the Saxons by a combination of military power and religious conformism. He subdued the Saxon tribes between 772 and 785, followed by Bavaria, before he turned his attention to Spain (785–801), a campaign that culminated in the capture of Barcelona in 801. Although he was unable to write (though he could read), his respect for learning was

genuine and he encouraged Alcuin and a community of
scholars in their Bible translation, teaching and writing.
The creation of a palace library, his support for reform
of the Frankish church and the beautiful artefacts that
survive from his court at Aachen show that this period
has deserved the title of the 'Carolingian renaissance'
of culture and learning.

In King Alfred the Great (849–99) Britain too
benefited from this Christian and Carolingian inheritance
later in the same century. Alfred, a more educated man
than Charlemagne, who himself translated Gregory the
Great's pastoral classic *Regula Pastoralis* for the use
of bishops and clergy of his kingdom, had the same
cultivating effect. A circle of scholars, translators and
copyists was formed at his court, who maintained
Christian learning and culture against a background
of Viking and Danish pressures.

Russia

The 9th and 10th centuries were important also for the
development of Russian Christianity. Russia was peopled
by northern tribes from Scandinavia who moved down the
great rivers Dnieper and Volga to the surroundings of the
Black Sea and the Caspian. Two heroic Greek missionaries
had undertaken embassies to the Khazar people at the
bidding of Patriarch Photius in Constantinople and the
emperor in 860. They were Constantine (826–69), later
named Cyril, and Methodios (c. 815–85). Now they were
asked to respond to a request from Ratislav, prince of
Moravia, for teachers. Constantine believed on principle
that the Slav peoples should have the Bible in their own
languages rather than, for instance, in Latin. He duly
translated the Gospels, daily services and the liturgy
(communion rite) of John Chrysostom (c. 347–407),
one of the great figures of the eastern church known as
'golden tongue' (Greek: *chrysostomos*) for his eloquent
preaching, for the use of the Slavs. Constantine had
composed a special script, Glagolitic, (Cyrillic script,

*'Let schools be
established in
which boys may
learn to read.
Correct carefully
the psalms… the
calendar… the
Catholic books.'*

CHARLEMAGNE ON
EDUCATION,
*ADMONITIO
GENERALIS*, CAP. 72

*'The Greeks took
us to their
church and we
did not know
whether we were
in heaven or
earth. We only
know that their
God dwells
among men.'*

VLADIMIR'S ENVOYS
ON THE GREAT
CHURCH OF
ST SOPHIA IN
CONSTANTINOPLE

named after him may not have been his creation, though contemporary with him). He and his partner Methodios completed the Slav Bible in 881.

From 870 Bulgaria and its king Boris became an important Slav kingdom to identify with Greek or eastern Christianity and after 900 Kiev became the cradle of Russian Christianity. A reigning queen there was baptized at Constantinople in 957; her grandson, Vladimir, seen still by many Russians as the founder of Russian Christianity, was baptized after marriage to a Christian princess, Anne, sister of the emperor, around 988. The Russian church identified with Constantinople and its tradition of eastern orthodoxy. It was to survive Mongol invasions and Muslim pressures from the Turks as an enduring Christian tradition of worship, monastic life and peasant piety, giving also national coherence and unity.

The impact of the monasteries

One of the methods by which Christianity spread and maintained itself in Europe was through monastic communities. Their origin, as we have seen, was in the Egypt of Antony around AD 300, conveyed to Europe by such figures as John Cassian (c. 360–440), who experienced monastic communities in both Egypt and the Holy Land before founding monasteries near Marseilles around 415. Nevertheless, the true founder of European monasticism was Benedict of Nursia (c. 480–550). Like Antony, he began as a hermit in a cave at Subiaco, but around 529, he moved with other monks to Monte Cassino, a magnificent mountain site, which, because of its strategic eminence, was to be the scene of fierce fighting in the 1940s battle for Italy.

Benedict formed his rule for his own monks, which has been praised for its balance, moderation and stability. It is based on the call to obedience (to God but expressed also through the rule of the abbot), chastity and poverty, there being an absolute ban on ownership of possessions. The basic provision of daily chapel services (seven during the

Opposite page:
**Altar icon of
Saints Cyril and
Methodios, in the
Chapel Tower,
Trojan Monastery,
Bulgaria.**

day and two at night), combined with set hours for manual work, meals and study has met the demands of many communities for a balanced Christian life. In so far as the Benedictine ideal of dividing daily life by set times of prayer was also taken up by the non-monastic or 'secular' priests, Benedict may be judged to be the individual who has shaped the spirituality of western Europe.

In considering what became a dominant tradition, it is important not to forget the very different Celtic monasteries with their clusters of small beehive-shaped huts in stone or timber, often at remote spots lashed by the Atlantic as at the Irish site of Skellig Michael. According to Kenneth Clark, the art historian, such communities were vital centres of civilization as Viking looting, killing and destruction engulfed much of northern Europe.

Hundreds of Benedictine monasteries spread across Europe, with Christianizing effect, between 700 and 1000. In 910 an important monastic foundation was created at

Rule of Benedict

The Abbot and the Brethren

III. 'Whenever matters of importance have to be dealt with in the monastery, let the abbot summon the whole congregation and himself put forward the question that has arisen. Then, after hearing the advice of the brethren, let him think it over by himself and do what he shall judge most advantageous. Now we have said that all should be summoned to take counsel for this reason, that it is often to the younger that the Lord reveals what is best. But let the brethren give advice with all subjection of humility, so as not to presume obstinately to defend their own opinions; rather let the matter depend on the abbot's judgment, so that all should submit to whatever he decide to be best… let no one in the monastery follow his own inclinations and let no one boldly presume to dispute with his abbot…'

XXII. How the monks are to sleep: 'Let them sleep in separate beds and let their beds be suitable to their manner of life, as the abbot shall appoint. If possible, let them all sleep in one room… let a candle be kept burning in the cell until morning. Let them sleep clothed, girdled with belts or cords – but without knives at their sides lest they injure themselves in sleep. And let the monks be always ready; and when the signal is given, let them rise without delay and rival one another in their haste to the service of God… let not the younger brethren have beds by themselves but dispersed among the seniors. And when they rise for the service of God let them gently encourage one another, because the sleepy ones are apt to make excuses.'

Cluny in northern France, from which a reform movement was launched to renew the Benedictine communities. For some, however, this Cluniac reform was not enough and a fresh foundation at Citeaux, near Dijon in France, provided a more austere model with a stricter observance of the Benedictine rule. Between 1100 and 1400 these Cistercian foundations grew to number 694 communities and produced in one of their abbots, Bernard, abbot of Clairvaux (1090–1153), one of the outstanding figures of the medieval church. A product of Citeaux, he was the ally and critic of popes, a preacher of the second crusade and a writer of Christian theology and devotion. The hymn 'Jesu, the very thought of thee', attributed to him, may not be his composition, but its expression of warm devotion to the person of Jesus was of the kind for which he stood.

Scandinavia

This account of the Christianization of Europe by AD 1000 has shown something of the struggle to evangelize pagan tribes. A further example, ending in the collapse of Christian hopes, was in Scandinavia. Here, the great pioneering missionary, Anskar (801–65), a monk from modern France, founded the first church in Stockholm; he had already been expelled by pagan tribes from the area known as Schleswig-Holstein. He was responsible later for the conversion of Erik, king of Jutland in Denmark, but despite the efforts of a lifetime of missionary work in the Scandinavian countries there was a relapse into paganism after his death.

In Sweden an English monk, Sigfrid, re-established Christian mission and baptized King Olov around 1000. It took a further two centuries for Christianization to be complete.

In Norway, two Christian monarchs, both converted from the lives of Viking raiders, made a Christian impression on their people. Olav Tryggvasan (king of Norway 995–99) had a memorable meeting with a Christian hermit in the Scilly Isles, when still a Norse raider. Olav Haraldsson (c. 995–1030), king of Norway from 1016 to 1028, adopted a strongly Christian stance, which provoked much resistance. Denmark, partly due to the efforts of Anskar and an ally in the Danish chief, Harold, who had been baptized while visiting the Frankish court, became Christian effectively by 1035, over a century after Anskar's death.

Progress was often slow, there were frequent lapses into heathenism and in the very far north the Lapps (Sami people) remained unevangelized for centuries. Norwegian missionaries reached Iceland in Olav Tryggvasan's reign (following earlier Irish hermits) and Christianity replaced paganism there, the home of the earliest parliament, the Thing, in the early 11th century. In Greenland, Vikings led by Erik the Red had been exiled from both Norway and Iceland and Christianity advanced in the 11th century there, too, through the adherence of Erik's son, Leif.

Norsemen may have reached Newfoundland and North America long before Columbus. Their own community in Greenland received a bishop as head of the community in 1123.

Later developments

The final 500 years covered by this chapter saw a number of important developments in the Christianization of Europe. Various popes strengthened the hold of the papacy on the church and over political authorities. Europe has been left an indelible example of the growth of the spiritual power of the papacy under Gregory VII (d. 1085), known also as Hildebrand: threatened with excommunication and with it the dispensing of his subjects from their oaths of allegiance, Henry IV, the emperor, stood for days with his family in the snow at Canossa in 1017, until the pope relented.

Innocent III (1160–1216) proved an even more able and far-sighted pope. He asserted successfully the papal right to approve the appointment of emperors and, as we shall see, strengthened the church through his wisdom in patronizing the new orders of Franciscan and Dominican friars, the kind of fresh departures that a less visionary church leader might have stifled.

Before 1500 the papacy was to suffer various indignities, including exile in Avignon between 1309 and 1377 and schism, with one pope vying with another claimant for authority; but Hildebrand and Innocent III had strengthened its hold on church and rulers considerably.

The church was also largely responsible for the flowering of Europe's universities. Bologna, Paris and Oxford were founded before 1200 and by 1400 there were over 40, a number of them being in France, Italy and Germany, two in England (Cambridge was founded in 1209) and two in Scotland. Christian theology held a central place, along with law, medicine and the arts.

Friars: Franciscans and Dominicans

Two men were responsible for the creation of mendicant (begging) orders. Francis (1181–1226), who has arguably left a deeper impression than any Christian since apostolic times, was the son of a wealthy Italian textile merchant from Assisi. After living the life of a polished young man of privileged background, he felt increasingly called to a life of compassion for people like the beggars he met in Rome when on pilgrimage and the leper he embraced in order to overcome his fear of leprosy. Disowned by his father, he responded to the call to total poverty when hearing Christ's words to the rich young man of the Gospels (Mark 10:17–22). He collected 12 followers, an apostolic band, and secured approval from Innocent III to form an order in 1209. The friars were sent out to preach in pairs. Francis himself tried unsuccessfully to make his way to Muslims in North Africa through France and Spain in 1214–15, but he did succeed in visiting the sultan in 1219. In an era of crusades, he believed in dialogue and persuasion of Muslims. His order grew rapidly in his lifetime. It was to provide many adventurous and heroic missionaries of the Roman Catholic church, whether in China, Latin America, California, India or Africa.

'Those who have now promised obedience shall have one gown and those who really need them may wear shoes.'

RULE OF FRANCIS

A women's order, founded by Clare (1193–1253), was another result of Francis's teaching, known popularly as the 'poor Clares'. Later a so-called 'third order' developed, whereby lay people could associate themselves with the order.

Dominic (c. 1172–1221) was a Spaniard, born near Castile. Like Francis, he had shown his care for the poor during conditions of famine that caused him to give up his possessions. His call to mission preaching was in the context of the church's attempts to persuade the

Ramon Llull (c. 1233–c. 1315)

Bishop Stephen Neill has described Ramon Llull as 'one of the greatest missionaries in the history of the church'. Llull was a layman from Majorca, who married and lived the life of a knight and courtier until the age of 30. At this time he had a vision of Christ crucified, which caused him to consecrate his life to Christian mission, in particular towards Muslims, who had ruled Majorca for centuries but whose rule had now ended. Llull studied Arabic and sought the support of popes and royal courts in Aragon and France for his plans towards Islam. He succeeded in receiving royal support to establish a centre in Majorca for Franciscans to study oriental languages. He himself made three missionary journeys to North Africa to preach in dangerous circumstances. He was successful in establishing the study of oriental languages in the universities of Paris, Oxford, Bologna and Salamanca and in obtaining support for his missionary objectives at the Council of Vienne in 1311–12. His overall aim was to bring Christian, Muslim and Jew together from a basis of shared monotheism, 'that in the whole world there may not be more than one language, one belief, one faith', to which end his life and writings were devoted. He is respected still as a contemplative and mystic and joined the third (tertiary) order of the Franciscans. His last visit to North Africa may have resulted in his death from injuries sustained in the cause of his mission.

Opposite page:
Manuscript
illumination from
*Vida Cotidiana
Breviculum* of
the journey,
stoning, and
imprisonment of
Ramon Llull.

Albigensians, a deviant movement in the south of France, to return to orthodoxy. Again, Innocent III was responsible for persuading Dominic and his fellow missioners to adopt a rule and become an Order of Preachers between 1216 and 1218. Where Francis had somewhat distrusted learning, as distracting from simplicity of life, the Dominicans had an intellectual interest from the first. Certain of them made notable contributions to the universities of Europe. Albert the Great (Albertus Magnus, d. 1280), who taught in

The spread of the Cistercian order and the development of universities

- Cistercian monastery founded between 1100 and 1200
- University founded between 1150 and 1300
- University founded between 1300 and 1400

NORWAY

SWEDEN

SCOTLAND

DENMARK

NORTH SEA

ENGLAND

GERMAN EMPIRE

FRANCE

Citeaux

Cluny

ITALY

Monte Cassino

SPAIN

MEDITERRANEAN SEA

Cologne and Strasbourg among other places, was a leading Dominican scholar, and the greatest of all, who left an indelible mark on western and Roman Catholic theology, was Thomas Aquinas (c. 1225–74).

He was an Italian from Aquino in the kingdom of Naples from an aristocratic family, who taught at Cologne and Paris. His great work *Summa Theologiae* was a compendium of theology written for his fellow friars and is still influential. His own and his order's missionary vision was expressed in the *Summa contra Gentiles*, written to assist Dominicans in their work among non-Christians. Like the Franciscans, the Dominicans supplied the church with ready and adventurous pioneers in far-distant China and the East as well as in Europe. Their concentration was on study and preaching. In England they were know as the Black Friars to distinguish them from the Franciscans – they wore a black mantle over a white habit.

Monasteries, popes, universities and preaching orders all contributed strongly towards the Christianization of Europe. In addition, it is impossible to neglect the psychological effect of the amazing outburst of Gothic architecture that resulted. Cluny itself possessed the largest abbey church in Europe, over 400 yards (365 metres) long and 100 yards (90 metres) wide, mostly built between 1050 and 1110, though the abbey had been founded in 909. What must have been the effect on the ordinary man or woman to see structures of the size of Westminster Abbey (where the new nave was completed around 1085), Ely Cathedral (begun in 1080), Lincoln Cathedral (begun in 1086), or Durham, built in a single lifetime between 1098 and 1140 in England? Or the wonders of Chartres (1130–1230), St Denis in Paris (consecrated in 1144) and Vézelay, not to mention the glorious but imposing structures of the monastic foundations at Citeaux (1098), Clairvaux (1115) and, in England, at Rievaulx (1131) and Fountains Abbey (1132), all Cistercian foundations? The spread of such imposing

'All I have written seems like so much straw compared with what I have seen and what has been revealed to me.'

THOMAS AQUINAS, AFTER A SPIRITUAL EXPERIENCE IN THE LAST YEAR OF HIS LIFE (1273–74)

Map opposite: The original Benedictine monastery was at Monte Cassino. Major reforms of Benedictine communities took place at Cluny, but more austere reforms were put in place at Citeaux, which became the model for Cistercian communities.

stone constructions was matched across northern Europe by thousands of village churches before 1500, many of them miniature masterpieces of design and craftsmanship by stonemasons and carvers of genius. Wordsworth's 'sermons in stones' spoke of nature's appeal: but these buildings proclaimed the strength, creativity and often soaring aspirations of medieval Christendom. They preached as eloquently to those who saw them as St Sophia, the great Byzantine church of the 530s, had done to its Slav visitors in the 10th century.

The power and wealth of the church led, however, to both corruption and envy before 1500. For an institution founded on apostolic poverty, its landholding, the lifestyle of many of its office-holders and its social and political influence led to unease and unrest. Signs of dissatisfaction among churchmen themselves pre-date the Reformation and Martin Luther. John Wycliffe (c. 1330–84), a Yorkshireman by birth and Oxford don by profession, was Master of Balliol College, Oxford (1360–61) and an intellectual critic of medieval theology. A somewhat opaque person to understand, Wycliffe believed before his time in the translation of the scriptures into the tongue of the people and a return to primitive Christianity from contemporary abuses. His approach was popularized by Wycliffite preachers, the Lollards, many of whom were vigorously persecuted by the church authorities, though Wycliffe himself died naturally as rector of Lutterworth.

In Eastern Europe, a more influential figure was Jan Hus (1372–1415) in Bohemia. He became a great preacher and critic of abuses in what is now the Czech Republic, who, as rector of the University of Prague, knew and translated Wycliffe's writings and propagated his views. Church authority was sufficiently alarmed to put Hus on trial in 1414 and he was burned at the stake in 1415. It was an example of the power of the church leading to intolerance of ideas seen as subversive on such matters as property holding. In time, these attitudes led to the much

greater intellectual and spiritual explosion of the
Protestant Reformation.

Were this a conventional church history, men such as
the great Dutch scholar Erasmus (c. 1466–1536), with his
influence on New Testament scholarship and Christian
humanism; Martin Luther (1483–1546), German scholar,
monk and reformer, remembered for his 95 theses pinned
to the door of the church at Wittenberg in 1517 and his
rediscovery of justification by grace through faith; and
John Calvin (1509–64), humanist, French prose stylist
and systematician, author of the *Institutes of the Christian
Religion*, who made Geneva a centre of theology and
who influenced the Netherlands, France (the Huguenots),
Germany and Scotland would all feature as leading
thinkers. For this book, however, as important as these
towering individuals of the 16th century are men such as
Prince Henry 'the Navigator' (1394–1460), who prompted
the Portuguese exploration of Africa; Vasco da Gama
(c. 1460–1524), who reached India; and Christopher
Columbus (1451–1506). For with these Europeans of
the age of exploration went also the Christian faith as
Franciscans, Dominicans and later Jesuits and members
of other orders sought to propagate the faith to the Indies
(East and West), in North and South America and in Africa.

CHAPTER 4

Africa

Norrth Africa has already been noted as one of the cradles of Christianity, with Tertullian, Cyprian and Augustine of Hippo among the great Latin Fathers of the faith. Egypt too was highly influential, not least through the lives of the 'desert fathers' such as Antony and Pachomios. In this chapter, the rooting of African Christianity in Ethiopian Orthodoxy will be outlined. This highly indigenous form of Christian faith and practice has survived until today with an estimated 36 million adherents. We will then consider the pioneering efforts of the Portuguese captains, inspired by Henry the Navigator, which resulted in early penetration of the continent and the extraordinary story of the Christian kingdom of Kongo after 1487. The churches of the Reformation then attempted to convey the faith to Africa – Anglicans and Methodists in West Africa; Moravians, Dutch and other Protestants in South Africa; J.L. Krapf in East Africa; and the epic journeys of David Livingstone in central Africa. Later came the influence of Cardinal Lavigerie and the White Fathers and of Anglicans in Uganda. And finally the whole stirring story of Madagascar, which laid hold of the imagination of the Victorian public only a little less than Livingstone himself.

Ethiopian Christianity

An Ethiopian appeared early in Christian documents through the vivid story in Acts (8:26–40) of the eunuch and treasurer baptized by Philip the evangelist. The beginning of the Ethiopian church, however, is thought to have resulted from the influence of an enslaved captive, Frumentius, around AD 300. Frumentius was captured while on a trading voyage and taken to the local king in Axum. Here he helped the government and was allowed to leave around 340. He presented himself to Athanasius, then bishop of Alexandria according to the historian Rufinus (345–410), who, hearing of Ethiopia's need, consecrated him as bishop of Axum. Thus began a long tradition, whereby Ethiopian Orthodoxy looked to Alexandria and its Egyptian Coptic church until as recently as 1959. Alexandria provided the church's leader, the 'abuna', an arrangement that made for great difficulty and a shortage of clergy when the appointment of an ordaining abuna was delayed. Frumentius's work is said to have been furthered by the 'Nine Saints' from Syria around 480, who extended Christian life and became greatly revered in the Ethiopian church. Ethiopia became a Christian kingdom, which in many periods of historical upheaval remained focused on the Christian monarch up to the times of Haile Selassie in the 20th century.

Next pages:
Church of Pan
Bendito, Lalibela,
Ethiopia.

Certain characteristics of Ethiopian Christianity deserve to be noted. It was an extremely Jewish form of Christian tradition and for long periods observed the Sabbath rather than Sunday (and at one point both). It shared with the Falasha Jews great respect for the history of King Solomon and his visitor, the Queen of Sheba; and there was a tenacious legend that, after their meeting, the Ark of the Covenant had been procured from Jerusalem and taken to Ethiopia. This resulted in miniature 'arks', called the 'tabot', being displayed in places of worship. The classic account of the royal meeting is the document known as the *Kebra Nagast*, which may date as early as the 6th century. Ethiopian Christians saw themselves as Jews, having a Jewish inheritance, before they were Christians. They retained the practice of circumcision as well as practising baptism. Monarchs regarded their dynasty as from Solomon and in modern times one of Haile Selassie's titles was 'Lion of Judah'.

The Ethiopian church also had a strong monastic

*'From your lips
sweeter than the
scent of myrrh...
came forth books
from Arabic
to Ge'ez.'*

ON THE BIBLE
TRANSLATOR,
ABUNA SALAMA
(1348–88), IN THE
SYNAXARION

*'At length
the sheep of
Ethiopia, freed
from the bad
lions of the West,
securely in their
pastures feed.'*

POPULAR CHANT
AGAINST THE
CHURCH OF ROME,
C. 1640

tradition. The 'Nine Saints' were said to have founded
a number of communities around Axum, among them
Dabra Damo, which lasted 1,000 years; and around 1270
a famous monastery, Dabra Libanos, became a centre
of renewal. Axum itself had a very large, five-aisled
cathedral, but this was destroyed in a Muslim jihad in
the 16th century. At this point the whole kingdom could
have become Muslim permanently had it not been for
Portuguese military assistance in a decisive battle of 1543.
Much credit for the survival of Ethiopian Orthodoxy
has been given to their ancient translation of the Bible
into Ge'ez; their strong musical tradition in worship
maintained by the laity; and the deeply indigenous
Ethiopian and African character of their worship and
church life.

Helped by various Roman Catholic agencies, notably
the Capuchins and Jesuits, they have nevertheless
resisted attempts to align the church with Rome.

The extraordinary persistence of Ethiopian
Christianity with, among other symbols, its rock-hewn
underground churches from the reign of Lalibela
(1190–1225) and its colourful processions is underlined by
the fate of another flourishing Christian kingdom of the
8th to the 12th centuries in Nubia. This was a territory
around modern Khartoum, whose bishops were also
consecrated by the patriarch of Alexandria but were
indigenous to Nubia. It had a cathedral at Faras and, like
Ethiopia, the monarch was central to religion. In this case,
inheritance by a Muslim king led to the demise of Nubian
Christianity. This had dated from a mission initiated by
Emperor Justinian and his wife Theodora in 543 in
Constantinople; but by 580 the whole population had
followed their rulers into Christian faith. We know of a
bishop of Qasr Ibrim as late as 1372; but by 1500 the area
was Muslim and what had been a flourishing church
gradually disappeared. Excavations in the 1960s, prior
to the flooding of northern Nubia for the Aswan dam,
revealed the rich remains of Nubian churches.

The kingdom of Kongo

Portuguese progress down the west coast of Africa
resulted in trading forts at Elmina on the Gold Coast
(Ghana) in 1482 and expeditions up the River Zaire
by Diego Cao in 1483, 1485 and 1487. After a further
expedition in 1491, the local king, Mbanza Kongo, was
baptized as Joao I, after the reigning Portuguese king
(Joao II). Christianization proceeded apace under the king
Mvemba Nzinga, renamed Afonso (1506–43), who made
Christianity the religion of the nobility, taking their titles
of marquises etc. from the Portuguese aristocracy of the
day. In the capital of Sao Salvador there was an influential
Portuguese presence of about 100 traders. Afonso's son,
Henrique, was sent to Lisbon for education and made a
bishop in 1521; but he died soon after his return to Africa
in 1530. Afonso made frequent appeals to the king in
Portugal for assistance in establishing Christian faith and
life from 1514 onwards. A Portuguese priest of the time
has left a vivid, if hagiographic and idealized, portrait of
this African monarch, still regarded in Congolese tradition
as 'apostle of the Kongo'. We are told that he preached to
the people with great skill and clarity, a tradition of royal
preaching confirmed elsewhere. Father d'Aguiar described
him 'not as a man but as an angel sent by the Lord to this
kingdom to convert it, especially when he speaks and
when he preaches… better than we he knows the
prophets and the gospel of our Lord Jesus Christ'.

After the death of this remarkable African convert in
1543, the story of Kongo is one of missed opportunities.
Many Spanish Capuchins offered to go to Kongo after the
foundation of the Propaganda de Fide in Rome in 1622 as
a means of directing missionary orders, but the Portuguese
resisted any Spanish incursion. Jesuits based in the
Portuguese territory of Angola at Loanda offered help and
there were some indigenous priests including canons of
the cathedral in Sao Salvador. The Jesuits opened a
seminary there in 1624. There was even a visit from a
Kongolese ambassador to the pope, commemorated in

*'At Mbanza Zolu
I sent word to
the king to tell
the fetishists
to stop their
dances... I beat
the heads of two
idols... and
threw them
into the fire.'*

DIARY OF
FR CALTANISETTA,
CAPUCHIN
MISSIONARY IN THE
KONGO KINGDOM
OF THE 1690S

frescoes in the Vatican library, but no sooner had this African met the pope, Paul V, than he died while still in Rome in 1608. The Portuguese hold was broken in 1640 after their defeat by the Dutch and a party of Capuchins led by Bonaventura d'Alessano began 200 years of mission in 1645; but of the original party many died within two years and others were withdrawn on grounds of ill health. Some Capuchin help continued from a base in Loanda but by 1700 the Christian presence in Kongo, even in the most favourable area of Soyo, was fading. It would take the introduction of Baptist missionaries in the Congo of the 1870s in the shape of men such as George Grenfell (1849–1906) and Holman Bentley (1855–1905) to cause the king, Pedro V, to recall the nation's Christian past.

West Africa

By the late 18th century the trade in slaves from West Africa to the new world ran into thousands. After the successful campaign for abolition led by William Wilberforce and Thomas Clarkson, with the help also of a remarkable African in England, Olaudah Equiano, a British naval squadron patrolled off the slaving coast from 1807. The Portuguese were still exporting many thousands across the Atlantic to the slave fields of Brazil, as the English had done to the sugar plantations of the West Indies by the notorious 'middle passage', the noxious holds of the slave ships that caused so many to die in transit. One early governor of Sierra Leone, Zachary Macaulay, father of the historian T.B. Macaulay, actually experienced the horrors of the middle passage for himself. It was Sierra Leone that provided the answer as to what to do with the 're-captives' of the slave trade. The 'province of freedom' became a dumping ground for the navy's spoils from the slavers. The English Church Missionary Society, founded the same year as Zachary Macaulay became governor in 1799, continued its work there after Sierra Leone became a crown colony in 1807. By 1860, some 60,000 recaptured slaves had been landed through Freetown. Uprooted from their tribal structures, they were gradually settled in what in some cases became model Christian villages. One such was Regent, where the German-born missionary, W.A.B. Johnson (1787–1823) was pastor. An early recruit to CMS, Johnson was one of a number of his countrymen willing to serve with CMS at a time when home-grown missionaries were hard to find.

'We looked more to Mr Johnson than to Jesus.'

A SIERRA LEONEAN CHRISTIAN OF REGENT AFTER W.A.B. JOHNSON'S DEATH, 1823

One unexpected injection to Christian life in Sierra Leone was the arrival of 1200 freed American slaves. These organized themselves into 15 ships at Halifax, Nova Scotia, and arrived singing hymns as they came ashore with their Baptist, Methodist and other pastors, some from the so-called Countess of Huntingdon's Connexion, leading them. In time, Methodist life was greatly strengthened by the arrival from England of Thomas Birch Freeman (1806–90), the son of an African father and English mother, previously head-gardener at a Norfolk country house before becoming a missionary with the Wesleyan Methodist Missionary Society in 1837. He was able to survive the West African climate, which was fatal for many European missionaries, and gave long service in West Africa.

Some of the re-captives in Sierra Leone caught the vision of returning to their own tribal people with the Christian gospel. Among them was the Yoruba-born Samuel Adjai Crowther (c. 1806–91). Crowther had been recaptured from the Portuguese slaver *Esperanza Felix* in 1821. He became one of the first students at the new CMS college at Fourah Bay, later associated with the University of Durham for the granting of degrees in 1876. Crowther became a missionary to his own branch of the Yoruba, the Egba, in the 1830s, while also translating books of the New Testament into Yoruba. Crowther's friend and mentor in London, Henry Venn (1796–1873), secretary and chief executive of CMS, like the American Rufus Anderson (1796–1880) of the American Board of Commissioners for Foreign Missions, sought to create indigenous churches

Mary Slessor (1848–1915)

Mary Slessor is said to have learned some of her toughness as
a missionary pioneer by leading a group of youngsters in a
Christian youth club in Dundee. Her father was often drunk
and Mary, like David Livingstone, worked in a mill while still a
child. She was accepted for missionary service by the United

Presbyterian Church in 1876
and sent as a teacher to
Calabar, teaching in Duke Town
and Creek Town. She moved
to work alone among the
Okoyong people, saving twins
from their traditional fate of
death and making a home
for them and tribal women.
She lived very simply, settled

Mary Slessor.

quarrels and, as a consular agent of the Niger Protectorate,
administered justice. She was an example of identification and
cultural adaptability as a missionary, responsible for a whole
people's adherence to Christianity.

that were 'self-supporting, self-governing and self-extending',
leading in Venn's thinking to the *euthanasia* of the mission.

In 1864, Venn persuaded a reluctant Crowther to
become bishop on the Niger to mark the crown of Venn's
endeavours to build the 'native' or indigenous church in
West Africa. Although the decision was to lead to great
heartache for Crowther, Bishop Bengt Sundkler, himself
both bishop in Africa and a leading historian of its church
life, wrote of it: 'This appointment was one of the most
far-sighted ecclesiastical decisions in African church
history.' In the Roman Catholic world, the Jewish convert
and mission inspirer, Francis Libermann (1802–52), leader
of the Holy Ghost Fathers, sought an indigenous African
church in a similar way.

The Anglican CMS was perhaps the leading Christian

influence in West Africa (although the Scotland Presbyterian mission of Hope Waddell and Mary Slessor in Calabar deserves mention), but it was the Netherlands Missionary Society and the London Missionary Society (LMS) that provided some great pioneers in South Africa, by then Dutch-controlled. Moravian Christians formed a model Christian community at Genadendal under Georg Schmidt (1709–85), which is still a place of peace, tranquillity and sense of order today.

South Africa

Johannes van der Kemp (1747–1811) was a founder of the Netherlands Missionary Society. He had been a soldier and became a qualified doctor before arriving in Cape Town in 1799. He was a brilliant man, who upset conventional Boers with his marriage to a Malagasy slave girl, and his opposition to slavery and to the oppression of African peoples. The LMS also provided some great figures. Robert Moffatt (1795–1833), who arrived in Cape Town in 1817, John Philip (1775–1851), who came two years later and David Livingstone (1813–73). Moffatt, like

Portrayal of Genadendal, South Africa, the site of a Moravian mission.

T.B. Freeman, had been a gardener, coming from Overtoun in Scotland. He gave 50 years to mission north of the Orange River, mostly based at his station of Kuruman from 1821. His daughter Mary married Livingstone; and Moffatt guided Livingstone in his early years in the field. John Philip, also a Scotsman, in his case from Aberdeen, was sent by LMS as a mission administrator. He was an ordained Congregationalist minister, who combined work for the mission with a pastorate of a Congregational church in Cape Town. He, too, like van der Kemp, was

David Livingstone (1813–73)

Livingstone was born in the mill town of Blantyre, near Glasgow, Scotland. Having left the Kirk (the Church of Scotland), his father, Neil, brought up his family in an independent congregation in Hamilton, which resulted from the evangelical revival. As a boy, after a 12-hour day in the mill, Livingstone was offered two hours' schooling, during which he studied such texts as Virgil and Horace. In his twenties, he was fired by stories of Karl Gutzlaff's work in China, and in 1837, he offered himself to the LMS and trained as a missionary and a doctor. After a meeting with Robert Moffatt, during the Opium War in China, he decided for Africa. He qualified as a physician in Glasgow in 1840 and arrived in Cape Town in 1841, before joining Moffatt, whose daughter, Mary, he married. Their first child died in 1846 and they lost another child in 1850. During the period after 1852, Mary took the family to Scotland, but this proved a very unhappy episode, when her relationships with Livingstone's parents became strained, and she herself resorted to drink in her loneliness. After Livingstone's epic journeys of 1853–56 and his triumphant reception in the home counties, they were reunited. Mary accompanied him on his Zambezi expedition of 1858, but she died during it. Livingstone's eldest son, Robert, died in 1864 as a soldier in the Union cause (the abolition of slavery) during the American Civil War, a cause close to his father's heart. Livingstone was found by H.M. Stanley in 1871 and died in May 1873. His funeral, paid for by the government, was held in Westminster Abbey on 18 April 1874, with two royal carriages for the principal mourners, who included Moffatt, two of Livingstone's sons, Tom and Oswell, and his daughter, Agnes, to whom he had been particularly close in his last years.

a doughty opponent of what he saw as white oppression of the black population and like the Dutchman aroused deep hostility among Boers and other colonialists, including the British, for his political stance for indigenous Africans.

David Livingstone was the child of a poor home in Blantyre, Scotland. He worked in a cotton mill for 13 years before offering for missionary service and qualifying as a doctor in London. He joined Moffatt at Kuruman and spent 11 years with him (1841–52). Here he conceived his plan of exploration, which took him west to the Loanda

Print of David Livingstone reading the Bible.

Henry Morton Stanley (1841–1904)

Stanley is known to missionary history for his famous greeting of 1871, 'Dr Livingstone, I presume?' He had been born in Denbigh, North Wales and brought up in a workhouse before emigrating to the United States in 1858. He became a journalist and the *New York Herald* sent him in search of Livingstone. The story made him famous. In 1875 he visited the Kabaka of Buganda, Mutesa, and published an appeal for missionaries to be sent to Uganda, which prompted the CMS mission of 1877. Later, Stanley played a part in opening up the Belgian Congo to Christian missionaries when employed by Leopold II, the king of the Belgians.

'I go back to Africa to try to make an open path for commerce and Christianity. Do you carry on the work which I have begun!'

DAVID LIVINGSTONE
AT THE UNIVERSITY
OF CAMBRIDGE, 1857

coast of Angola and east to the mouth of the Zambezi at Quelimane, journeys achieved between 1852 and 1856. The extraordinary physical and geographical feat made him a hero in Victorian Britain. He had a triumphant tour, which included an enthusiastic reception at the Senate House in Cambridge, where his inspiring address effectively launched the Universities' Mission to Central Africa.

Two other missions of note also took their inspiration from Livingstone. The Free Church of Scotland's Livingstonia Mission was launched in 1875 and, soon after, the Church of Scotland began its Blantyre Mission south of Lake Nyasa, both missions being in modern Malawi. It was during yet another daunting journey of exploration that H.M. Stanley, representing the *New York Herald*, found Livingstone at Ujiji in 1871. Two years later, in modern Zambia, Livingstone finally died in May 1873. There followed one of the great African epics, when his two helpers, Susi and Chuma, carried his body at great risk to themselves over hundreds of miles to the coast. Livingstone was buried finally in Westminster Abbey on 18 April 1874.

Debate about Livingstone will continue. Was he a missionary or an explorer? How far was his hope of

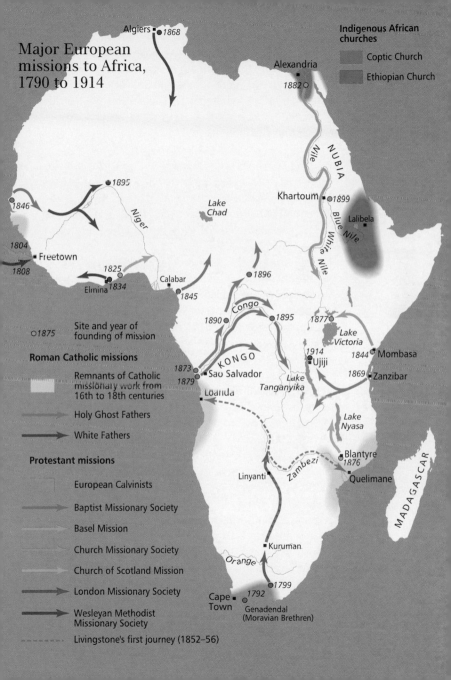

Major European
missions to Africa,
1790 to 1914

Indigenous African churches

Coptic Church

Ethiopian Church

Algiers *1868*

Alexandria
1882

NUBIA

Nile

Lake
Chad

Khartoum *1899*

Lalibela

Blue Nile

White Nile

1895

Niger

1846

1804
Freetown
1808

1825
Calabar
1834
Elmina *1845*

1896

Congo
1890 *1895* *1877*

Lake
Victoria

1914
Ujiji

1844 Mombasa

1869 Zanzibar

KONGO

1873 Sao Salvador
1879
Loanda

Lake
Tanganyika

Lake
Nyasa

MADAGASCAR

○*1875* Site and year of
founding of mission

Roman Catholic missions

Remnants of Catholic
missionary work from
16th to 18th centuries

Holy Ghost Fathers

White Fathers

Protestant missions

European Calvinists

Baptist Missionary Society

Basel Mission

Church Missionary Society

Church of Scotland Mission

London Missionary Society

Wesleyan Methodist
Missionary Society

Livingstone's first journey (1852–56)

Blantyre
1876
Quelimane

Linyanti
Zambezi

Kuruman

Orange

Cape
Town
1792
Genadendal
(Moravian Brethren)

1799

opening up the interior of Africa to commerce and civilization as an antidote to the slave trade a legitimate and reasonable aim? What of his treatment of Mary and his family in his single-minded pursuit of his goals? Such issues cannot be handled here, though they will continue to fascinate and perplex. C.P. Groves, a widely versed historian of Christianity in Africa, wrote of him:

The great trans-continental journey... was an achievement that marks a watershed in the history of the continent and... meant more for the expansion of Christian missions in Africa than any other single exploit. It was a breaking of the lock that opened a door inviting advance...

Or, in Livingstone's own words, 'The end of the geographical feat is the beginning of the missionary enterprise.' What is clear is that Livingstone, unlike many Europeans, had an instinctive affinity with Africans based on mutual respect, eliciting extraordinary loyalty and enduring friendship in response.

East and Central Africa

The Portuguese had taken Mombasa in 1591 and there had been some Christian penetration by the Augustinian order, some of whom became martyrs, leading to African converts in the early 1630s. Protestant work had to wait until J.L. Krapf (1810–81) arrived there in 1844. Krapf was another German recruit to the CMS, who had been sent first to Ethiopia. He lost both his wife and infant daughter in Mombasa and was joined in his lonely service by another German, Johannes Rebmann (1820–76), with whom he became the first European to see Mount Kenya. To this Rebmann added Kilimanjaro in 1848. Both missionaries studied Swahili and Rebmann translated the Gospels of Luke and John. North of Lake Victoria lay the kingdom of Buganda in modern Uganda. Here too the CMS gained entry in 1877, not least in the person of the Scottish engineer and lay missionary, Alexander Mackay (1849–90).

'Tell our friends that in a lonely grave on the African coast there rests a member of the mission.'

J.L. KRAPF TO CMS
FROM MOMBASA,
1844

Islam was also present, introduced by Arab traders. Uganda occupied the mind of one of the greatest Roman Catholic missionary strategists and animators in Cardinal Charles Lavigerie (1825–92), then archbishop in Algiers. He was founder of the Missionaries of Our Lady of Africa, known as the White Fathers. In 1878, a party of them came to the kingdom led by Father Lourdel. The Baganda and the reigning Kabaka, Mutesa (d. 1884), proved open to the missionaries and many of the young men, who, as king's pages, lived in close proximity to the court, became Roman Catholic and Anglican Christians. Mutesa's successor, Mwanga, had learned homosexual practices from the Arabs and he became enraged that Christian youths would not participate in his tastes. A number of 'boy martyrs' were speared to death in 1885. Anxiety about Christians acting as a potential fifth column in a threatening situation may have contributed to a fresh atrocity in 1886, when 32 men were burned to death. There was much jostling for position by Muslims, Roman Catholics and Anglicans in the years that followed but through the intervention of Captain (later Sir)

Cardinal Lavigerie in an Algerian camp for orphans in 1867.

Frederick Lugard, acting for the Imperial British East Africa Company, a decisive victory at Mengo in 1892 led to a British protectorate in 1893. The colonial period that followed was a time of mass response to Christianity in the country.

Before turning to Madagascar, certain general comments about Christian advance can be made. First, as the cases of Mutesa and Mwanga indicate, the response of rulers to the missionaries and their message could be all-important. Moffatt had a strong relationship with the Ndebele chief, Mzilikazi, while his successor, Lobengula, another astute and powerful chief, prevented the great

Francois Coillard, missionary to the Sotho people of modern South Africa and Lozi people of modern Zambia. Portrait with his wife.

François Coillard (1834–1904)

Coillard was born in Asnières-les-Bourges to a French Huguenot family. He arrived in Cape Town in 1857. He spent 20 years in Leribe in Sotho territory, where his missionary work was interrupted by Boers. In 1877 he tried to reach further north but was arrested by Lobengula. While in the chief's custody he

learned of the Lozi people in modern Zambia. He was refused entry at first in 1878 by chief Lewanika but reached the territory in 1886. Lewanika used his good offices to approach Queen Victoria for a treaty, which was achieved in 1890. Coillard was invited to become a British resident but refused. His wife, the daughter of a Scottish minister in Edinburgh, whom he married in 1861, died in 1891 but Coillard continued and greatly reinforced the mission with another 15 missionaries in 1898. One of Lewanika's sons became a Christian. Coillard was one of the most outstanding of all missionaries to Africa in a remarkable group from the Paris Evangelical Mission.

Moshoeshoe I (1786–1870)

Moshoeshoe was paramount chief of the Sotho people. After the clans had been dispersed by the victories of Chaka and his Zulus, he welded them together and resisted the efforts by the Boers and the British settlers to deprive his people of territory. Ultimately he sought and gained protection from the British for Lesotho in 1868. He had permitted the Paris Evangelical Mission to introduce Christianity in 1833, allowing traditional ways to be reformed and adapted while avoiding communal upheaval. Eugene Casalis became his friend and adviser. Moshoeshoe died the night before his public baptism was to take place.

French missionary, François Coillard (1834–1904), from advance. Nevertheless, Coillard, Eugene Casalis and Adolphe Mabille of the Paris Evangelical Mission were very influential, not least through Casalis's relationship with the great Sotho chief, Moshoeshoe, and Coillard's with Lewanika, chief of the Lozi people in modern Zambia.

The Zulu leaders, Dingane and Cetshwayo (the latter imprisoned by the British in 1879) were not responsive to the missionaries, although among them they had one of the most radical and imaginative representatives of Christianity in Bishop Colenso (1814–83). His ideas on the Bible caused great anxiety at home but to the Zulus he was 'Sobantu', the father of the people. After his death, his daughters, Harriette and Frances, continued his campaign for Zulu rights. Livingstone was able to baptize a chief in Sechele of the Kwena people, though he later withdrew his support over marriage discipline. Polygamy in Africa was a continual problem to the missionaries.

In a different case, not involving a chief, van der Kemp's lasting influence was seen through the conversion of the African Ntsikana (1760–1820), whose hymn-writing and profound reinterpretation of Christianity in African terms meant much to the Xhosa and Khoi peoples. Robert Lawes (1851–1934) of the Livingstonia Mission established

'If I adopt your law I must entirely overturn all my own and that I shall not do.'

CHIEF NGQIKA OF THE XHOSA PEOPLE TO VAN DER KEMP, 1799

a strong relationship with Mbelwe, chief of the Ngoni.

Africans showed themselves responsive to the education offered by the missions at institutions like Lovedale, where James Stewart presided, and none more so than the ordained African Tiyo Soga (d. 1871), as influential in the south as that product of Fourah Bay, Samuel Crowther, had been in the west. These and others were a standing contradiction to Europeans who maintained that it would take generations of 'civilization' to produce an educated African leadership.

Madagascar

As in South Africa, it was the LMS who provided the missionary pioneers to the Malagasy people in the early 19th century. Portuguese religious, Jesuits and Lazarists, had made attempts between 1587 (a Portuguese missionary was killed after brief service in that year) and 1674; but the first churches were founded by David Jones (1797–1841) and Thomas Bevan of the LMS, between 1818 and 1835. They did their work well. For a period of intense persecution followed under Queen Ranavalona (reigning 1828–61), with Malagasy Christians hurled to their deaths over precipices or burned or stoned.

Incoming Holy Ghost Fathers and Jesuits were forced to keep to the coastal areas. The constancy of Malagasy Christians caught the imagination of the missionary public and provided an example (which modern China reproduced after 1949) of the removal of expatriate missionaries leading to considerable indigenous growth – often to the surprise of the missionary agencies. After 1860 other Protestant missions entered, among them Norwegian Lutherans in 1866. Madagascar became a French colony in 1896 and the LMS, whose churches at their peak had a membership of some 300,000, looked to the French Paris Evangelical Mission to assist them, with its fluent French-speakers. Although at first the colonial administration was anti-clerical, Roman Catholic advance was considerable, with much work done by the Jesuits.

'Christians had been speared, smothered, starved or burned to death, poisoned, hurled from cliffs or boiled alive in rice pits.'

B.A. GOW, WHO
ESTIMATED 150,000
DEATHS, 1979

Today some 44 per cent of Malagasays are Christian, while most others follow traditional religions.

Before leaving 19th-century Africa, it is important to emphasize that the spread of Christianity was again and again an indigenous African enterprise, independent of the missionary. Sometimes it could result from the dynamism of a particular people like the Mfengu, who initiated Christian response in different areas. Sometimes it resulted from African clergy and missionaries like the Sierra Leoneans. Sometimes it was the direct effect of gifted individuals like the prophetic figure of Ntsikana among the Xhosa and, as will be seen in the final chapter, Prophet Harris on the Ivory and Gold Coasts. Africans began to look to indigenous forms of Christianity, independent of European influence. One such pioneer of what became known as 'Ethiopianism' was Mangena Mokone, originally an ordained minister in the Wesleyan Methodist church, who became dissatisfied with the paternalism of the missionaries. This led him to found an 'Ethiopian' breakaway church, which was given formal recognition by the Boer leader, Paul Kruger, in the Transvaal as 'the Ethiopian Church of South Africa' in the 1890s. Ethiopianism and 'Zionism' (African charismatic groups with emphasis on healing) have led in the 20th century to large numbers of African Independent Churches (AICs), a phenomenon that will recur in the final chapter.

CHAPTER   5

America

T he expansion of Christianity after Columbus's
epoch-making voyages of the 1490s to the Caribbean
and what is now known as Latin America was
heavily dependent on the two great colonial powers of
Spain and Portugal. From the beginning there was a
religious intention to the efforts of the conquistadors,
however subordinate it may have become to conquest and
treasure-seeking for themselves and their royal masters.
By means of the papal bull *Ceteris Partibus* of 1493 (such
documents being known by the initial words of the Latin
text) the pope, Alexander VI, divided the world between
the two spheres of influence. Although the map was
altered later to enable Portugal to colonize Brazil, the
original division was along a line drawn from the North
to the South Pole west of the Azores, with Spain given the
West Indies and the Americas; and Portugal, which had
already explored the west coast of Africa in the time of
Henry the Navigator (1394–1460) and moved towards India
through Vasco da Gama (c. 1460–1524), Africa, India and
the East. Priests accompanied da Gama's voyages and
they were equally part of Spanish colonization, combining
the roles of missionaries, explorers, secretaries and
chroniclers. Often they belonged to religious orders,
Franciscans and Dominicans at first and later, with special
missionary emphasis and success, the Jesuits.

*'It is the Holy
Trinity in his
infinite goodness
who has led your
Highnesses to
this enterprise
of the Indies.
The Trinity has
made me his
messenger.'*

COLUMBUS ON HIS
THIRD VOYAGE
OF 1498

Latin America

It was then with a sense of religious mission, as well as
the motivation of acquiring wealth from the indigenous
peoples, that men like Cortes (1485–1547) and Pizarro
(c. 1475–1541) began their conquest of the Aztec and
Inca empires. As in the case of Charlemagne, the goal of

Christianization, if achieved by enforced baptisms at the point of the sword, appeared not to trouble the consciences of these military leaders. Cortes was born in Medellin in Spain. He attended the University of Salamanca and left Spain for Cuba in 1511. At the age of 33 he mounted an expedition against the Aztec capital in Mexico with 700 fellow Spaniards, equipped with canons and muskets, reinforced by thousands of Indian allies.

Although he experienced a reverse after a massacre of Aztec nobles and temporarily had to withdraw from the capital, Tenochtitlan, he returned to the city in August 1520 and systematically destroyed it. He founded and built Mexico City on the same site. He became governor of New

Portrait of Francisco Pizarro by Jean Mosnier.

*'Or like stout
Cortez, when
with eagle eyes/
He stared at the
Pacific – and all
his men/ Look'd
at each other
with a wild
surmise –/ Silent
upon a peak in
Darien.'*

JOHN KEATS, 'ON
FIRST LOOKING INTO
CHAPMAN'S HOMER'

*'Tell me, by what
right or justice
do you keep
these Indians
in such cruel
and horrible
servitude… are
they not men?'*

ANTONIO DE
MONTESINOS IN
A SERMON, 1511

Spain and captain general of the forces in 1522, titles that were confirmed by the emperor, Charles V, when Cortes returned to Europe in 1529. He was later replaced by a viceroy and died in 1547. His contemporary, Pizarro, directed his attention to the Inca empire in Peru. He obtained authority from Spain for its conquest in 1528–29 and attacked the Incas in 1530. Again a massacre of Incas assembled at Cajamarca was followed by the capture of the Inca capital of Cuzco in November 1530.

The period of the conquests, which included success in Columbia (1536–38) but failed in Chile, was followed by ecclesiastical and colonial consolidation. Under the so-called *padroado* (Spanish: *patronato royale*) the papacy devolved on the monarchs of Portugal and Spain all the ecclesiastical patronage and appointments in Latin America. The appointments to the new bishoprics of Tlaxcala (1525) and Mexico City (1526), as of Lima (1541) and Caracas, were royal choices. Another of Alexander VI's bulls allowed the monarchs to collect tithes in their colonies and so to finance further Christianization in 1501 (*Eximiae devotionis*); in 1508 a bull (*Universalis ecclesiae*) enabled them to determine the territorial areas of the bishoprics and the naming of all candidates from bishops to curates.

On the colonialist front, a system was developed with the title of *encomienda*. By this method, a number of Indians were assigned to a colonist or landlord. He was ascribed rights to both tribute and labour but it was understood that he was responsible for the Christianizing of those committed to his charge. In fact, however well-intentioned, the *encomienda* system became a by-word for oppression and cruelty by the colonists or *encomenderos* and soon resulted in the virtual slavery of the Indians after its introduction in 1503. Brave Dominican priests denounced the system, one of the earliest protestors being Antonio de Montesinos (c. 1486–c. 1530) on the island of Hispaniola in 1511.

Another Dominican, whose father had accompanied Columbus on one of his voyages, Bartholemew de las Casas

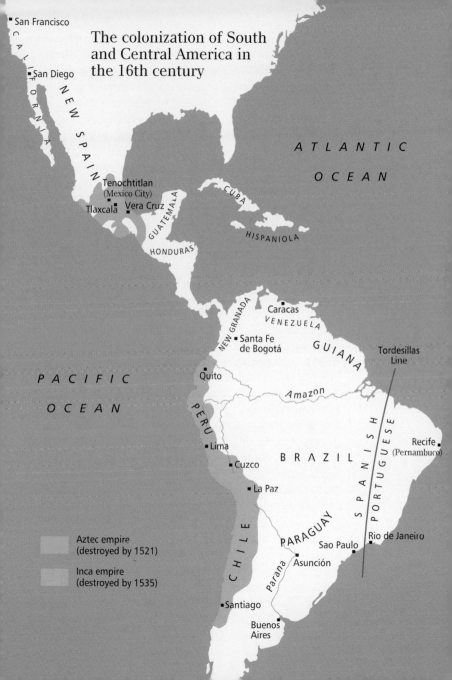

The colonization of South and Central America in the 16th century

San Francisco

San Diego

CALIFORNIA

NEW SPAIN

Tenochtitlan
(Mexico City)

Tlaxcala

Vera Cruz

GUATEMALA

HONDURAS

CUBA

HISPANIOLA

ATLANTIC

OCEAN

NEW GRANADA

Caracas

VENEZUELA

GUIANA

Santa Fe
de Bogotá

Tordesillas
Line

Quito

Amazon

PACIFIC

OCEAN

PERU

Lima

Cuzco

BRAZIL

La Paz

CHILE

PARAGUAY

Parana

Santiago

Asunción

Sao Paulo

Rio de Janeiro

SPANISH

PORTUGUESE

Recife
(Pernambuco)

Buenos
Aires

Aztec empire
(destroyed by 1521)

Inca empire
(destroyed by 1535)

*'God created
these simple
people without
evil and without
guile... nor
are they
quarrelsome,
rancorous,
querulous or
vengeful.'*

BARTHOLEMEW
DE LAS CASAS
ON INDIANS

(1484–1566), witnessed the burial alive of an Indian leader in Cuba. He became a champion of Indian rights for 50 years from 1514. Confronted by a philosophical position, rooted in the study of Aristotle, that viewed the Indians as slaves by nature, an inferior race intended for their menial role, he worked tirelessly in America and Spain to change attitudes and convince those in authority that the use of force was contrary to apostolic understandings and that the Indian should be respected as God's creation. His efforts to lobby support at home in influential circles, which received recognition from the emperor, Charles V, against the activities of the colonists, included a debate in 1550 at Valladolid with the Aristotelian philosopher and scholar, Sepulveda. Before he died, de las Casas's campaign for just laws for the Indians had been largely responsible for the New Laws of 1542–43, which prohibited Indian slavery and caused the Council for the Indies to be reorganized. After serving as bishop of Chiapas (1544–47), de las Casas used his pen on behalf of the Indians, most famously in his *Brief Account of the Destruction of the Indies*, a hard-hitting critique of Spanish practice, in which he was held to have exaggerated abuses in a work widely disseminated in Europe.

Jesuit missions

The Franciscans and Dominicans had been first in the field among the orders from 1510 onwards; but in the second phase of the mission the Jesuits were active, in Brazil from 1549, in Peru from 1567 and in Mexico from 1572. José de Anchieta (1534–97) was one great Jesuit missionary who gave 44 years of his life and became known as the 'apostle of Brazil'. He was one of the founders of both the Sao Paulo and Rio de Janeiro Jesuit missions. Another heroic figure and defender of Indian rights in Brazil was the Jesuit, Antonio Vieira (1608–97), who opposed the Inquisition and the colonists equally, was admired by John IV of Portugal but almost lynched by the colonists in 1661 after the king's death.

In the 17th century, Jesuits were active in Bolivia,

Spanish colonial empire in Latin America. Painting of Dominicans baptizing Indians, Castillo de Chapultepec, Mexico.

Uruguay and Paraguay. In the early 1600s they created a missionary system known as the 'reductions', which was pioneered among the Guarani people in Paraguay but later extended to other missions. By 1623 they had created 23 settlements among the Guarani, which aimed both to protect them from colonists and to Christianize them. In total these communities comprised some 100,000 people. Each settlement had a church, school and workshops and led an ordered life, with work being obligatory for Indians, who, however, had free time and their own gardens

José de Anchieta (1534–97)

José de Anchieta was born in the Canary Islands and studied at Coimbra at the Jesuit College, entering the order in 1551. He reached Brazil in 1554 and co-founded a mission in the Indian village of Piratininga with his Jesuit superior. Ultimately this village became Sao Paulo. He learned the Tupi-Guarani language and taught both Guarani and Portuguese children. He wrote the first grammar and dictionary of the Tupi language, and he is regarded as the father of Brazilian literature. He became Jesuit superior of the Sao Paulo–Rio de Janeiro mission and from 1577–87 provincial of Jesuits in Brazil.

allotted to them as well as set periods of service to the general community. The colonists resented the removal of the pool of labour from their control but the Jesuits resisted their influence.

General agitation against the Jesuit order in Europe and in the colonies led to their expulsion from Portuguese territory in 1759 and from Spanish possessions in 1767. The order was suppressed in 1773. All this proved a disastrous blow to the reductions as a means of evangelization. It also exposed the weakness of a form of mission that was essentially paternalist, with little or no authority passed over to the indigenous people or attempt to develop Indian ministry. With the removal of the Jesuit leaders the reductions collapsed as a system and whole villages were engulfed by jungle after 150 years as oases of Christian community.

Modern Venezuela became an area for further Jesuit exploits. They penetrated the jungles of the Amazon to reach large numbers of Indians. The area of the upper Amazon valley was known as the Maynas. One early Jesuit pioneer, Rafael Ferrer, began a mission in 1599 that cost him his life in martyrdom in 1611. Further Jesuit efforts achieved more and by 1661 many thousands were baptized in this area. The Jesuits found that these people were less easily led than the Guarani people and there was opposition from the Portuguese; but with assistance from

The Mercedarians

The Mercedarians were a Spanish order, dating from around 1235. Their original aim was the collection of money to ransom captives and redeem properties that had fallen into Muslim (Moorish) hands in Spain during its occupation by the Moors from around 750 to 1250. In origin it was a lay order but clergy were admitted and controlled the order in the 14th century. Members travelled to Muslim lands to seek freedom for Christian captives. Gradually academic theology and educational work was included in its work and an order of nuns was founded. Peter Nolasco (c. 1180–c. 1249) its founder was canonized in 1628.

Franciscans, some half a million people were reached in the Maynas region.

Central America
Central America was again pioneered by the orders – Franciscans, Dominicans and Mercedarians. The first church on the isthmus of Panama was built in 1510. Missionaries entered Guatemala in 1526, and de las Casas, who had joined the Dominican Order in 1522, introduced other Dominicans to Nicaragua. Guatemala had 22 Franciscan and 14 Dominican houses by 1600.

Mexico, after the era of Cortes, again attracted the orders, so that Franciscans landed at Vera Cruz in 1524, Dominicans in 1526, Augustines in 1533 and later Capuchins (1565) and Jesuits (1572). A Franciscan, Juan de Zumarraga (c. 1468–1548), became bishop of Mexico City in 1528 and proved to be a firm defender of Indian rights and a believer in an indigenous clergy, towards which he used his college at Tlatelolco. He became archbishop of Mexico in 1546. The University of Mexico, founded in 1553, reflected the church's emphasis on education. In the north of the country a famous Jesuit missionary, Eusebio Kino (1644–1711), Italian by blood but born in the Swiss Tyrol, arrived in Mexico in 1681 and did missionary work in lower California, in the modern state of Arizona and in Colorado. Described as a modest, gentle, humble man who was an upholder of the welfare of Indians, he travelled perpetually in the interest of the mission. He had hoped to reach the war-like Apache people but death intervened in 1711. Before their dissolution the Jesuits achieved another 37 stations in Lower California by 1767.

In the modern state of California a string of Franciscan missions are still to be found between San Diego and San Francisco. Father Juniper Serra (1713–84), born in Majorca, became the leader of the mission and founded such communities as Monterrey and Carmel (1770), San Luis Obispo (1772), Santa Barbara (1786), still an impressive and active Christian community, and others. By 1800 some

100,000 Californian Indians, many from the Chumash people, had been reached by the mission and some 18 Franciscan mission compounds established. At least some of the thrust to the north was driven by Spanish fear of Russian incursion, moving south from Alaska. Father Serra also spent some years establishing work in Texas.

Martyrdom of three Jesuit priests in 1642: Frs Brébeuf and Lalemant at the stakes, Fr Jogues kneeling. Alfred Pommier (1802–40).

Canada and Alaska

Russians were not the only European power to be feared by Spain. The French had American possessions in Louisiana and French Jesuits were active in the Mississipi valley. Some dreamed of

Jean de Brébeuf (1593–1649)

Jean de Brébeuf was born to a family of the French rural nobility and entered the Jesuit order in 1617. He reached Canada in 1625. He learned one of the Algonquin languages and lived among the Huron people of the north-west, adding their language and staying for three years (1626–29). After capture by the British, he returned to France but renewed his mission in Canada from 1633. He founded the mission 'St Marie among the Hurons' in 1639, destroyed by Iroquois warriors in 1649. He was tall and strongly built and became known as the gentle giant. Like the Jesuits in Paraguay, he favoured withdrawing the Hurons into a missionary settlement. He is an example of the heroic pioneer Jesuit, whose missionary life ended in martyrdom in the field.

a link between French Canada and the south down this waterway. Father Marquette (1637–75), a gifted linguist, moved down the Mississipi from the north and attempted a mission among the Illinois Indians. While based in Quebec he had made himself master of seven Algonquin

*'We folded our
hands and
venerated the
Cross in the
presence of a
large number of
savages in order
to show them...
that our
salvation
depended only
on the Cross.'*

JACQUES CARTIER IN
CANADA, 1534

languages and he gained a considerable reputation as
an Indian-style orator. He was in turn preacher, pastor,
explorer and geographer, whose writings contributed to
local knowledge of Indian peoples and horticulture. In
the political struggles of the day, the French were to lose
New Orleans and West Mississipi to Spain and Eastern
Mississipi to the British; but French Carmelites,
Recollects (a 16th-century branch of the Franciscans)
and Jesuits achieved much in the French possessions
before the Jesuits' expulsion in 1763. French Jesuits had
attempted but failed in a mission to the Sioux but in
Canada French Roman Catholic influence remained
strong. The explorer Jacques Cartier had placed a cross
when on an expedition to Canada in 1534–36 and then
arranged for three native Canadians to be baptized on his
return to France.

In 1611 two Jesuit missionaries settled in Canada but
their mission ended with an English attack. In Quebec,
the Recollects began work in 1615. An outstanding priest,
Joseph le Caron, began among the Huron people, who
were mainly situated north of Lake Ontario, between
Georgian Bay and Lake Simcoe, down the St Lawrence
River from Quebec and Montreal. They numbered around
20,000 at the time. François de Laval, a missionary-minded
vicar apostolic in Canada (vicars apostolic being Roman
Catholicism's representative figures before dioceses are
formed) became bishop of Quebec in 1674. He was a
founder of the Société des Missions Étrangères of Paris,
and he gave a fresh impetus to mission by linking his
seminary in Quebec to the society in Paris.

Jesuits, who had favoured his appointment, had
begun work among the Hurons, chief among them being
Jean de Brébeuf (1593–1649). He had learned the Huron
language between 1626 and 1629 but was taken prisoner
by the English before returning to the Huron mission in
1633–34. This mission was tragically overwhelmed by the
war-like Iroquois in 1649 and he and another Jesuit leader
of 'St Marie among the Hurons', Gabriel Lalemant, were

captured and tortured to death by the victors. Both martyrs were canonized by Pius XI in 1930. Quebec was the scene of a further initiative in 1639, when a wealthy noblewoman, Madame de la Peltrie, was instrumental in French nuns, Ursulines, opening a school for native Canadian girls. This was a successful piece of missionary work by women.

The British General Wolfe secured Canada, after his victory over the French General Montcalm on the 'Heights of Abraham' of Quebec in 1759; and in 1763, at the Treaty of Paris, Canada became British. At about this time the Jesuits, on the verge of their dissolution, expanded their work among native Canadians and Americans to include various sub-groups of the Iroquois in the Mohawks, the Oneidas, the Cayugas and the Senecas, as well as working among the Algonquins at Sillery near Quebec and a related clan, the Abenaki. But the missions struggled with Iroquois resistance, problems of disease (introduced by the missionaries themselves), and the influence of brandy and other strong drink (also brought in by Europeans) to which the Indians became addicted. Although thousands of Iroquois were baptized, the large majority remained pagan. Bishop Laval was responsible for another famous Jesuit missionary, Claude Allouez (1622–89), initiating missionary work west of Montreal and north to Lake Nipigon in 1667. Jesuits

Ursulines

This order of nuns was founded in 1535. It developed into an educational order, working in girls' schools, not least in 16th-century France. Marie Guyard ('Marie of the Incarnation', 1549–1672), who founded the house in Quebec in 1639, was one of the most famous members of the order. She and two other sisters of the house in Tours, with Madame de la Peltrie, accepted the Jesuit invitation to assist the mission in Canada through a convent based in Quebec. Marie was the first superior of the Ursulines. She was also a religious visionary and mystic, whose letters and writings were published after her death.

reached the Hudson Bay area and baptized there. Even after the British had won Canada and their order had been suppressed in Europe, some Jesuits remained in Canada as late as 1789.

In the far north, Russians had entered Alaska in 1741. Russian Orthodox Christianity had begun work on Kodiak Island, off Alaska, in 1794. By 1796 some thousands of the islanders and the population of the Aleutian Islands had been baptized. They met hostility from the Russian American Company but the mission received fresh invigoration by the arrival of Innocent Veniaminoff (1797–1879), an Orthodox priest from Siberia, who reached the Aleutian Islands in the 1820s. He mastered the Aleutian dialect well enough to translate the Gospel of Matthew and to write a devotional tract that became a classic, *An Indication of the Pathway into the Kingdom of Heaven*. After working among the Aleutians for some years, he served among the Tlingit people. After his wife died, the Orthodox Church appointed him as bishop of an area that included California. Between 1840 and 1868 he continued notable work. Although 40 years of missionary service, often in conditions of great physical hardship, had left him exhausted and ready to retire, he was appointed metropolitan of Moscow, a position he used to found the Russian Missionary Society as a means of support for Orthodox missions. His outstanding service was recognized in 1977 by the Orthodox Church of America conferring on him the title of 'Evangelizer of the Aleuts and Apostle to America', while the Russian Orthodox Church made the 200th year of his birth (1997) 'the year of St Innocent'. Alaska was sold to the United States in the 1870s but the Holy Synod created an independent bishopric to include Alaska in 1872. By 1900 there were some 10,000 Orthodox Christians in the diocese. Of the 65,000 Alaskan and Aleutian people today, some 70 per cent claim to be Christian and many of these belong to the Orthodox community.

America and Protestant missions

Roman Catholic orders were often heroic pioneers in the
continent of America and from 1622 Roman Catholicism
had the great advantage of a central organizing body for
missions in the Sacred Propaganda for the Faith (today's
Congregation for the Evangelization of the Nations).
By contrast, the churches of the Reformation had
comparatively little missionary vision in the 16th century
and no directing agency in the 17th. French Protestantism,
led by the Huguenot Admiral Coligny, attempted a short-
lived experiment off Rio de Janeiro where Admiral
Villegagnon established a settlement with Calvinist worship
and church life at its heart between 1555 and 1560, until
the French were expelled by the Portuguese. A longer-
lasting Calvinist settlement was initiated by the Dutch after
their capture of Pernambuco, which remained Calvinist for

*The Arrival of the
Pilgrim Fathers* by
Antonio Gisbert
(1835–1901).

40 years. Jan Maurizius created a number of Calvinist centres in the north-west of Brazil, in what had been Portuguese settlements. Some 20 Reformed congregations developed in Brazil, with 50 pastors employed, one of the larger congregations being in Recife.

North America presented a different scene. The symbolic event of the voyage of the *Mayflower* with its 'Pilgrim Fathers' in 1621 was a historical pointer to the strong influence of Calvinist Protestantism in New England. The states of Massachusetts, Connecticut and New Hampshire were strongly Congregationalist and Presbyterian in church life and heavily influenced by English Puritanism. Some, at least, of these pioneering people felt a responsibility for spreading the Christian faith to the native American indigenous peoples.

John Eliot (1604–90) is regarded as the chief initiator, when acting as Presbyterian pastor of Roxby, near Boston in Massachusetts from 1632. He taught himself the Iroquois language, and, like the Jesuits in Paraguay but probably with no knowledge of them, founded 'praying towns',

Engraving of John Eliot preaching Christianity to Massachusetts Indians.

communities that, over 40 years, included over 3,000 Christian Indians in Natick and other settlements. Eliot translated both the New Testament (1661) and the Old Testament (1663) and showed far-sightedness in preparing an indigenous Christian ministry of native American preachers, of whom there were 24 by his death.

A remarkable family called Mayhew were also pioneers in missionary work, their field being Martha's Vineyard, Nantucket and the Elizabeth Islands off Cape Cod. Thomas Mayhew bought the islands in 1641 with an Indian population of around 5,000 people. His son, Thomas (1621–57), began a mission among them and by 1651 around 200 had responded to his work. After the death of both generations, John, youngest son of the younger Thomas, and his son Experience Mayhew (1673–1758) continued the mission, Experience having the advantage of fluency in the language and ability to write in it. Zechariah, his son, carried on a tradition that lasted from 1641–1806 and produced Indian clergy and one Harvard graduate. Of this family, Kenneth Latourette has written: 'Not even the line of Gregory the Illuminator in Armenia was so prolonged in its leadership.' Gregory's mission began in 280, and was continued well into the next century by his son, but was eclipsed by the Mayhews.

We have already mentioned the Moravian community in Georg Schmidt's mission at Genadendal in South Africa, but here we should note an early Moravian mission among Eskimo (Inuit) people in Labrador, as well as Moravian missionaries founding communities of Christian native Americans. (Their origins as a Christian community will be examined in the next chapter.) Their own leader in Europe, Count Zinzendorf, had been in North America in Philadelphia from 1741 to 1743 and prompted work among indigenous people and colonists alike. The leader in America became August Spangenberg (1704–92), who organized missionary preparation for Moravians at their centre at Bethlehem, Pennsylvania. A mission was founded in the same state named Gnadenhütten (dwellings of grace). David Zeisberger (1721–1808) gave a lifetime of missionary service from 1745, but disaster struck at Gnadenhütten when, in his absence in Detroit to convince the British of the neutrality of the mission, 96 of his Indian converts were massacred by American troops in 1782, innocent casualties of the war of American Independence. Zeisberger started again, giving a total of 62 years to missionary work, during which he mastered several indigenous languages and produced dictionaries and other essential linguistic aids.

David Brainerd
A New England figure who was to become a missionary icon to many, including William Carey and David Livingstone, was David Brainerd (1718–47). He was born in the farming

Lake
Nipigon

CANAD

OJIBWA

Lake Superior

ALGON

Lake Michigan

Lake Huron

HURON

Lake Ontar

St
Clair

Lake Erie

PENNSYL

■ Gnadenhütten

Sites of major settlements and
Protestant missions in north-
eastern America from 1600

VIRG

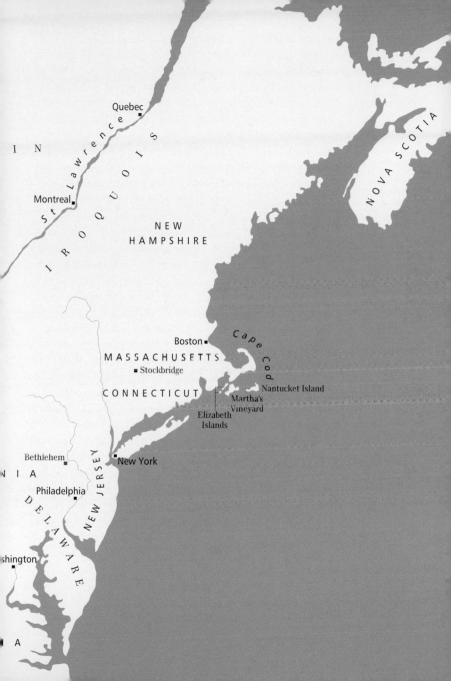

*'There is one
thing in Mr
Brainerd easily
discernible, that
is, that he was
one who by his...
natural temper
was... prone
to... dejection
of spirit.'*

JONATHAN
EDWARDS'S PREFACE
TO THE *ACCOUNT* BY
DAVID BRAINERD

*'Rode several
hours in the rain
through the
howling
wilderness.'*

DAVID BRAINERD ON
HIS WAY TO THE
DELAWARE INDIANS,
JOURNAL, 1 MAY 1744

country of Haddam, Connecticut and studied for the
ministry at the then Yale College, from which he was
somewhat unjustly expelled in 1741. He impressed the local
leadership of the Scottish Society for the Propagation of
the Gospel enough for them to employ him for missionary
service from 1742, when he worked among the Indians of
Stockbridge and then, after Presbyterian ordination, in
western Massachusetts, Pennsylvania and New Jersey. In
the last setting he experienced scenes of religious revival
among the Delaware Indians, which he recounted in his
journals, as well as his own spiritual history, with all its
fluctuations of mood in spiritual exaltation and despair.

Brainerd died young but his journals and the account
of his life by the great preacher and philosopher, Jonathan
Edwards (1703–58), became immensely influential in the
Protestant world. Edwards, also a student at Yale and citizen
of Connecticut, was himself a missionary at Stockbridge
among the Indians from 1750–58. His eminence as a leading
philosopher, theologian and president-elect of Princeton
lie outside the limits of this book, but he was one who
combined the life of scholarship with extensive efforts for
the Indians. His life of Brainerd was published in 1749.

The New England Presbyterians and Congregationalists
were not matched by other non-Roman Catholic churches
in their efforts among native Americans, although
Episcopalians and the missionary society of the Church of
England, the Society for the Propagation of the Gospel, did
achieve some work among native Americans. Work among
the Iroquois of New York was initiated by the then governor,
Lord Bellomont, and one converted Mohawk chief, Joseph
Brant, helped to establish a Mohawk church. Queen Anne
of England even presented some communion silver to four
Mohawk Christians in London in 1704 for use in her 'Indian
chappell of the Mohawks'.

In Virginia the royal charter declared one of the aims
of the settlement to be the conversion of the Indians.
The first minister of Henrico, Alexander Whitaker, did
act as a missionary and introduced the Indian princess,

Pocahontas, to the faith. A college was founded at Henrico for the education of Indians and there were appeals for funding for Indian missions at home by King James I and his archbishops, so that one of six professorships at the College of William and Mary was set apart for the teaching of Indians.

Methodists had behind them the experience of John and Charles Wesley when acting as Anglican priests and missionaries of the SPG in Georgia from 1735. John Wesley had sought to reach out to the Choctaw and Chickasaw peoples, despite being principally a chaplain to English settlers, but he had little response. After his breach with the Church of England over irregular ordinations, his chief lieutenant in the New World, Thomas Coke (1741–1814), became a driving force for Methodist missionary work, attempting a mission in Nova Scotia in 1786 before being deflected to the West Indies by his wind-driven ship. Methodist missions really came into their own in the 19th century after Coke's death and took the form of frontier preachers and 'circuit riders' under the direction of his great collaborator, Francis Asbury (1745–1816), who himself travelled some 300,000 miles (480,000 kilometres) on horseback in the cause of the gospel and whose vision included both native Americans and African Americans for Methodist outreach. By the time of Asbury's death in 1816 Methodist membership had moved from 13,000 in 1784 to 200,000, a sign of growing influence.

Expansion north

The 19th century in North America saw the further extent of the north reached by Roman Catholics, Anglicans and Methodists. Two priests reached Red River (Winnipeg) in 1818 and by 1843 a large number of people in the settlement became Roman Catholic Christians. The Order of the Oblation of Mary Immaculate (OMI) was assigned western Canada, and Albert Lacombe (1827–1916) became a leading missionary in the north-west, who won the confidence of native Canadians and was known as the

'To settle the State of Religion as well as may be for our own people... and then to proceed in the best methods... towards the conversion of the Natives.'

ANNUAL SERMON OF 1701 EXPRESSING THE AIMS OF THE SPG

'apostle of the Blackfeet' and by them as 'the man with the good heart'. In 1820, the Anglican CMS took responsibility for the evangelization of the west and the north. William Bompas (1834–1906) worked heroically among the people of the extreme north-west up to the Arctic ocean from 1862 and was consecrated bishop of Athabasca in 1874, publishing works in seven different Indian dialects. Most Eskimo (Inuit) people became Anglican in allegiance. They received their first bishop in Archibald Fleming (1883–1953) in 1933, who signed himself 'Archibald the Arctic', by which time 80 per cent were Anglican and 20 per cent Roman Catholic. In Labrador, where once again Moravians had been the pioneers, one losing his life in 1752, CMS took up the work in the person of Edmund Peck (1850–1924), previously a Royal Navy sailor for 10 years, who baptized some 100 Eskimos between 1876 and 1882. Methodists made contact with the people of the far north through their representatives at the posts of the Hudson's Bay Company after 1840, the most widely known missionary being James Evans (1801–46) among the Ojibwa people of St Clair River.

The 19th century was a period of extraordinary

James Evans (1801–46)

James Evans was born in Hull, England. In 1822 his family emigrated to Canada. After some years as a teacher he was converted at a Methodist camp meeting and began to teach Indian children at the Rice Lake school in 1828. His facility in language led him to construct an Ojibwa alphabet and syllabary and he translated scripture and wrote hymns in their language. In 1833 he was ordained into the Methodist ministry and was appointed to the St Clair River. After 1839 he travelled north of Lake Superior and applied his skill to the Cree language. He was involved in the tragic and accidental death of a teacher, Thomas Hassall, and returned to England leaving much creative work as his memorial. His *Cree Syllabic Hymnbook* of 1841, printed by his own hands, is thought to be the first book printed in the Canadian north-west.

development in North America, despite the ravages of the Civil War of 1861–65, especially in the United States. Great numbers of immigrants flooded into the country from Europe, estimated at 33 million between 1820 and 1950. Of British emigrants between 1815 and 1900, 65 per cent found their way to the USA. Of African Americans, whereas only some 12 per cent had belonged to any sort of church life in 1860, by 1910 the number was 44 per cent. Many joined the Baptist and Methodist congregations of the southern states after the abolition of slavery. In the nation at large, the extraordinary achievement to any non-American was the blending into one nation of so many disparate peoples, so that their American citizenship was more prominent than whether their roots were Italian, Irish, Jewish, German, Scandinavian or English. The influx posed great challenges to the churches but Americans became a church-going people. The treatment of native Americans, however, as of many slaves of African origin, had often been shameful.

There were many parallels in the treatment by the British of aborigines in Tasmania and Australia and the activities in Spanish, Portuguese and Dutch territories, where European ascendancy resulted again and again in oppression of indigenous peoples. As we have seen, from time to time brave missionary figures rose up in protest, like Bartholemew de las Casas or, in the previous chapter, John Philip in South Africa, to champion the rights of those suffering at the hands of the colonists. Yet in many cases these brave men were themselves subject to obloquy and social ostracism by people of their own race.

Sitting Bull (Tatonka Iyotake), a Hunkpapa Sioux chief victorious in the battle against American forces led by General Custer at the Battle of Little Bighorn in 1876.

'The Great Spirit has made the Red Man and the White man brothers and they ought to take each other by the hand... the White Man has robbed us.'

CHIEF SITTING BULL OF THE SIOUX TO QUEEN VICTORIA, 1877

CHAPTER 6

Europe from 1500 to 1900

The period after 1500 in Europe left it in the throes of the Reformation. The churches that resulted from this religious upheaval, Lutheran, Calvinist, Anglican, Anabaptist, had to devote their energies to their own church life. There was little to match the Roman Catholic outreach to the world through the orders, who accompanied the empire building of Spain and Portugal as Franciscans, Dominicans, Augustinians, Jesuits, Capuchins and others. In the last chapter we noted the exception to this Protestant vacuum in the French Huguenot settlement off Portuguese Brazil in the time of Admiral Coligny's leadership; and the Dutch efforts that resulted in Calvinist congregations in Penambuco and in the northeast of Brazil. The 17th century saw little change. John Eliot was an exception as a Calvinist pioneer in his work among the unevangelized native Americans. It was not, however, until the emergence of the Moravians that the churches of the Reformation developed missionaries with the kind of vision of Jesuits such as Francis Xavier (1506–52) and Robert de Nobili (1577–1656) or the kind of considered missionary strategy represented by the Propaganda (1622) under its Italian head, Francesco Ingoli, which will be examined in the next chapter.

Moravian missionaries

The Moravians had an interesting history. They originated as a reforming movement, which owed its impetus to Jan Hus, the Czech reformer, who was executed for pursuing a Wycliffite programme in 1415. A group called the *Unitas*

Fratrum, who stood in the Hus tradition, were greatly reduced in numbers in the 17th century in their native Bohemia at a time of Roman Catholic resurgence, known as the Counter Reformation. A German aristocrat, Count Nikolaus von Zinzendorf (1700–60), born in Dresden and in the service of the government of Saxony from 1722, welcomed the remnant of them on his estates. He had been influenced by the warm devotion to Christ in the movement known as Pietism in Lutheran Germany,

Portrait of Count Nikolaus von Zinzendorf, founder of the Herrnhut Brotherhood.

centred on the remarkable work of A.H. Francke (1663–1727), who founded the school Zinzendorf had attended and taught at the University of Halle. He also founded other institutions, including a large orphanage, and has led a recent historian of Pietism, W.R. Ward, to describe him as 'one of the great visionaries and... most remarkable organizers in the whole history of Christianity'.

Zinzendorf created a religious community on his estates known as Herrnhut. His interest in mission appears to have been inspired by seeing two baptized Greenlanders when attending the coronation of the king of Denmark in Copenhagen. He became a man of consuming missionary vision, often critical of what he saw as the dry orthodoxy of the Lutheran church. His ardour that Christians should win 'trophies for the Lamb' by the conversion of individuals was shared by the Moravian community.

Their very understanding of the church was that it be missionary. Christian life for believers was understood as a missionary calling for all. Although Zinzendorf laid emphasis on winning individuals, Moravian missions developed a strong and deep emphasis on Christian fellowship in community, with warmth of devotion and worship. As noted in previous chapters, Moravians reached

'The enthronement of the Lamb of God as the sole creator, sustainer, redeemer and sanctifier of the entire world.'

ZINZENDORF ON THE
MISSIONARY AIM

Nineteenth-century engraving of the university building in Halle.

South Africa in the person of Georg Schmidt (1709–85) in 1739, who created a Christian community at Genadendal; and among native Americans in North America through the work of the Moravian leader August Spangenberg (1704–92), and great missionaries like David Zeisberger (1721–1808) and the Christian Indian communities of the Gnadenhütten in Pennsylvania. Moravians strongly influenced John Wesley through their missionary Peter Böhler, during and after his service in Georgia.

Farflung Moravian missions were to be found in the West Indies (1732), Greenland (1733), Labrador (1752) and among Tibetan people. K.S. Latourette has written of the Moravians in his *A History of the Expansion of Christianity*:

Here was a new phenomenon in the expansion of Christianity, an entire community, of families as well as of the unmarried, devoted to the propagation of the faith. In its singleness of aim it resembled some of the monastic orders of earlier centuries but these were made up of celibates. Here was a fellowship of Christians, of laity and clergy, of men and women, marrying and rearing families, with much of the quietism of the monastery and of Pietism but with the spread of the Christian message as a major objective, not of a minority of the membership but of the group as a whole.

> *'On shipboard... it pleased God... to give me twenty-six of the Moravian brethren who endeavoured to show me "a more excellent way".'*
>
> JOHN WESLEY, *JOURNAL*, MAY 1738

A.H. Francke (1663–1727)

Francke was born in Lübeck and became a lecturer in Leipzig. He was deeply impressed by P.J. Spener (1635–1705) and his spirituality as an early leader of Pietism, who sought the renewal of the Lutheran Church while acting as court chaplain at Dresden. The University of Halle was founded through Spener's influence. Francke became professor of Greek and Oriental languages there in 1691, while also acting as pastor and preacher locally. As well as his orphanage he opened a poor school, a publishing house and a dispensary. He became professor of theology in 1698. He pursued Spener's aims of deepening Bible study, lay priesthood, the regulation of theology in the universities, the renewal of preaching and practical Christianity.

Before turning to the development of the Protestant missionary societies, which were to become so influential after 1800, certain other Protestant pioneers deserve mention. Hans Egede (1686–1758) was born in Norway. He became a Lutheran missionary in Greenland and a pioneer among Eskimo people there; it was two of the converts of this mission that Zinzendorf saw in Copenhagen. In Greenland the local shamans, known as *angakut*, were the dominant religious force but Egede secured a response to his work, not least through the care he and his wife exercised through a small-pox epidemic in 1733. Egede experienced some tensions with Moravian missionaries who arrived in that year but his son, who had been brought up in Greenland, mastered the language and produced a New Testament for Greenland in 1766. By then Egede had founded an institution for the training of missionaries in Copenhagen in 1736 and the work prospered.

Denmark, whose Lutheran church had been influenced by Pietism, was the country that sent out two other early pioneers to India – Bartholemäus Ziegenbalg (1682–1719) and Heinrich Plütschau (1677–1752) – both Germans and both educated at Halle. From Copenhagen they settled in the Danish settlement of Tranquebar as the first Protestant missionaries to India in July 1706. They were 'royal Danish' missionaries, with their salaries paid by King Frederick IV of Denmark. Both owed much to A.H. Francke but on arrival were wise enough to seek help with the Tamil language from Jesuit missionaries. Ziegenbalg produced the first Tamil New Testament in 1715. He died four years later, aged 36.

The Danish example of royal influence is a reminder of the kind of monopoly on all kinds of overseas enterprise that operated in Europe. In England, for example, such trading bodies as the East India Company or the Hudson's Bay Company, in an era of what became known as mercantilism, were granted monopoly trading agreements directly from the crown by royal charter. The same

Street Scene at the Harbour in Copenhagen by Sally Henriquez, 1844

*'Pietism caused
Germany to be
Protestantism's
leading
missionary
country... [and]
demonstrated in
a remarkable
way what total
dedication
meant.'*

DAVID BOSCH,
*TRANSFORMING
MISSION*

*SPG was to
'supply the want
of learned and
orthodox
ministers' in the
colonies and in
'factories beyond
the seas'.*

ROYAL CHARTER OF
WILLIAM III, 1701

principle held true for the Society for the Propagation of the Gospel (SPG), incorporated by royal charter in 1701.

As an economic system it was to be dissolved by the new economics of Adam Smith and his *Wealth of Nations* as part of the movement known as the Enlightenment in Europe, during which royal monopolies gave way to the kind of free economic competition of the new capitalism. The joint stock companies of the 19th century, with their boards of directors and basic voluntary principle, became a model for missionary societies, which stood in a voluntary relationship to their churches, as did the Church Missionary Society to the Church of England.

Despite its foundation date of 1701, SPG was not the earliest missionary society in England; that distinction belongs to the Society for Promoting Christian Knowledge of 1698. Like SPG it owed its existence to the vision of an English rector, Thomas Bray (1656–1730), who had himself acted for the bishop of London in seeking to meet the needs of the colonists of Maryland in 1699. SPCK and SPG were both active in North America and SPCK was prepared to employ German Lutherans, some ordained, maintaining strong ties with A.H. Francke and German Pietism, while also giving support to the Danish-Halle mission in Tranquebar where Ziegenbalg and Plütschau served. A series of German missionaries, often selected by Francke, went from Halle to this mission, of whom possibly the greatest of all was Christian Friedrich Schwartz (1726–98), who served in India for nearly 50 years (1750–98). Schwartz was influential in South India generally and was admired equally by the Hindu prince, Saraboji, and the East India Company, both of whom commemorated him with monuments in marble.

The era of voluntary societies

The end of the 18th century in England was a time of a fresh set of missionary initiatives through the foundation of the voluntary societies. Here were concentrated missionary-minded individuals, who formed organizations that, like the missionary orders of the Roman Catholic church, often acted independently, while still maintaining links with denominational churches. One of the first of these was the Baptist Missionary Society, which was organized to support the great Protestant pioneer William Carey in 1792. Carey and his Baptist co-workers, Joshua Marshman (1768–1837) and William Ward (1769–1823), with their base at Serampore, will feature in the next chapter, but it is interesting to note here that they sailed to India in a Danish ship because of prejudice against their aims in England and among the East India Company. Here was a clash between the royal charter monopoly and the voluntary missionary agent.

'Expect great things. Attempt great things.'

WILLIAM CAREY IN A
SERMON ON THE
TEXT 'ENLARGE THY
TENT' (ISAIAH 54:2)
AT NOTTINGHAM
TO THE
NORTHAMPTONSHIRE
ASSOCIATION,
30 MAY 1792

William Carey
with Brahmin
Pundit, an
Oriental
professor.

In 1795 the London Missionary Society (LMS) was founded. Although it had a Congregationalist core, it was non-denominational and open to evangelical membership from all churches, being committed to a policy that no particular form of church government would be pursued for its missions. It was the society that supported Robert Moffatt and David Livingstone in Africa and the lonely pioneer Robert Morrison (1782–1834), who retained a foothold in China from 1809, engaged in Bible translation. It was also to be influential in Madagascar and Oceania.

In 1799, evangelical Anglicans, many of whom had supported LMS, decided to form their own society, the Church Missionary Society (CMS). Like the SPCK, CMS found itself employing German Lutheran missionaries in its early days, when missionary recruits were hard to find. In its important early work among the freed slaves of Sierra Leone, it was a German missionary, W.A.B. Johnson, who was a typical if exceptional figure, as were the Germans J.L. Krapf and W. Rebmann in East Africa. Both SPG and CMS were active increasingly in areas of the British empire after 1800.

Missionary societies also developed in mainland Europe. Johannes van der Kemp (1747–1811), who has appeared in these pages as a pioneer in South Africa, was co-founder of the Netherlands Missionary Society in 1797, before arriving in Cape Town as a NMS missionary in 1799. In Basel, the German Christian Fellowship founded the Basel Mission in 1815 with C.G. Blumhardt (1779–1839) as its first director. It was in the mission seminary of this society that many of the early CMS missionaries received their training, Krapf and Rebmann among them. In all, the seminary supplied 88 of the early CMS missionaries. It was another indication of the close links between German Pietism and the English societies.

Germany also produced the Leipzig Society, whose first director was Karl Graul (1814–64), a notable missionary thinker; the Rhenish Society (1828), which worked in South Africa and elsewhere; the North German

Albert Schweitzer (1875–1965)

Schweitzer was the son of a Lutheran pastor in Alsace. He became famous both for his New Testament writings and his brilliant musicianship, not least his interpretation of J.S. Bach's organ works. In 1906 he published the German edition of *The Quest of the Historical Jesus* with its view of the subject as dominated by the end-time. It had a great impact on the theological schools of Europe and is still influential. In 1913 he decided to forsake the academy to work in Africa as a medical doctor and established a hospital at Lambarene in French Equatorial Africa (Gabon). This work was based on his principle of reverence for all life. Although linked to the Paris Society he provided his own support and sat loose to doctrinal orthodoxy. He was awarded the Nobel prize for his humanitarian efforts in 1953. The first of his books on his African experiences was *On the Edge of the Primeval Forest*.

Dr Albert Schweitzer pictured in 1933 with an African child at his hospital at Lambarene, Gabon.

Society (1836), which worked in West Africa; the Gossner Society (1842), with work in Bengal; the Herrmansburg Mission (1849), working in South Africa and British India; and the Neuendettelsau Society (1849), which worked in New Guinea and among Australian Aborigines. Among many great pioneers from these missions, particular mention is made later of Ludwig Nommensen (1834–1918), sent by the Rhenish Society to the Bataks of Sumatra; Christian Keysser (1877–1961) of the Neuendettelsau Society among the Kate people of New Guinea; and Bruno Gutmann (1876–1966), sent by the Leipzig Society to work among the Chagga people of Mount Kilimanjaro.

One famous German-speaking missionary from

Alsace, who chose to associate himself with a French society, was the renowned theologian and musician Albert Schweitzer. As a missionary doctor in West Africa at Lambarene his links were with the Paris Evangelical Missionary Society. This was founded in 1819 as an international and inter-denominational body. It was the society that gave much notable service in Africa through those outstanding Frenchmen mentioned earlier, François Coillard, Adolphe Mabille and Eugene Casalis. It took over much of the LMS work in Madagascar after 1896. The Scandinavian nations also developed missionary societies: the Swedish Missionary Society (1835); the Norwegian Missionary Society (1842); the Finnish Missionary Society (1859); and a further Swedish body, the Svenska Missionsforbundet of 1878, which broke away from the Church of Sweden and formed a free Lutheran church in that year. Swedish missions have worked in Ethiopia,

Nineteenth-century sketch of Dwight Lyman Moody, American evangelist and businessman.

D.L. Moody (1837–99)

Moody was born in Northfield, Massachusetts. He began work aged 17 in his uncle's shoe store in Boston. He did Sunday School and evangelistic work in Chicago from 1858 and acted as a YMCA relief worker during the US Civil War. He toured England, with Ira D. Sankey as organist and soloist, on an evangelistic journey in 1873–75, attracting very large crowds (the Sankey and Moody hymnbook dated from 1873) and returned in 1881–84 after a number of urban missions in the USA. In 1880 he founded the Northfield Conferences, at which many student participants discovered a missionary vocation. In 1886 the Student Volunteer Movement for Foreign Missions (SVM) was formed with its watchword 'the evangelization of the world in this generation'. He founded the Moody Bible Institute in 1889, which has been judged to have made a larger contribution to foreign missions than any other Protestant institution in the USA.

Zaire and Tanzania; and Norwegians in Madagascar and Zululand.

For Protestantism, the influence of Pietism and its propagation through Moravian missions provided one source of missionary stimulus. The evangelical revival, connected with the activity of John Wesley and George Whitefield, provided another. John Wesley's decisive spiritual experience of 1738 arose from his friendship with the Moravians and their roots in Pietism.

The Methodist Missionary Society can date its beginnings to 1786, although it began more formally in 1819. In the 19th century, fresh impetus was provided by the American preacher and revivalist D.L. Moody, who favoured inter-denominational evangelistic work, which in turn gave rise to missionary societies of this kind. Societies like the China Inland Mission, founded in 1865 by James Hudson Taylor, were an inter-denominational meeting ground of Baptists, Anglicans, Methodists and others. CIM may have been the largest of these societies but others like the Africa Inland Mission (1895) and the Sudan Interior Mission (1893) were similarly constituted, often known as 'faith missions' because of their policy and practice of making no public appeal for funds.

Although Roman Catholic missionary work had languished somewhat in the 18th century (one sign of which being the suppression of the Jesuit order in 1773), as with European Protestantism there was fresh infusion of missionary enthusiasm in the 19th century. The importance of Cardinal Lavigerie and his White Fathers has already been mentioned, but in addition the foundation of the Marists ('the Society of Mary') in Lyons in 1816, the Picpus Fathers confirmed by the pope in 1817 (both congregations active in the Pacific), the Holy Ghost Fathers ('Spiritans') in their merger with the Immaculate Heart of Mary in 1841, the Mill Hill Missionaries ('St Joseph's Society for Foreign Missions') founded by Cardinal Vaughan (1832–1903) in London in 1866 and the Society of the Divine Word (Societas Verbi Divini – SVD) in Steyl, Holland in 1875 were

'When I met Peter Bohler again he consented to put the dispute upon the issue I desired, namely scripture and experience... I felt my heart strangely warmed. I felt I did trust in Christ, Christ alone, for salvation.'

JOHN WESLEY,
JOURNAL, MAY 1738

all signs of renewed missionary vigour. French, English and Dutch orders were reviving the missionary vision of the Church of Rome during Latourette's 'Great Century' of Christian expansion.

Cultural impact and missionary thinking

Two final subjects deserve attention in this chapter. First, in this European missionary awakening, it can often seem that European culture and values (for example, Victorian English forms of clothing) were as important to the missions as the Christian gospel. Such a judgment has to be balanced, however, by the recognition that some of the profoundest understandings of alternative societies and peoples were provided by missionaries. So, a Jesuit like Jean de Brébeuf, through his extraordinary facility in the Huron language, provided the indispensable tools for the understanding of the Huron people; William Ward, companion of William Carey, produced a study of Indian language and religion *The History, Literature and Religion of the Hindoos* (1817–20) far ahead of its time as a study of an alternative religion; James Legge (1815–97), LMS missionary in China, was the leading Sinologist of his day, ultimately recognized for his expertise by an Oxford professorship in 1876; the missionary tradition produced anthropologists of world stature in Henri Junod (1863–1934) with his *Life of a South African Tribe* and R.H. Codrington (1830–1922), who produced ground-breaking studies like *The Melanesians* when working for the Anglican Melanesian Mission. Again and again it was missionary translations, dictionaries and tribal descriptions that laid the groundwork for wider cultural studies. Much sensitivity to language and culture accompanied much insensitivity in the inculturation of the Christian gospel.

Secondly, the 19th century in Europe was also a time of development in reflection of the theory and practice of mission and its subjection to a fresh analysis. Propaganda in Rome had reflected fruitfully on mission for the Church of Rome since its inception in 1622, some of the results of which will appear in the next chapter. In Protestant circles Gustav Warneck (1834–1910) established mission studies, becoming the first professor of mission at Halle, which had provided so much of the vitality of Protestant missions after 1700. Reflection on the indigenous church as the goal of mission, to be 'self-supporting, self-governing and self-extending' came from mission directors such as Henry Venn of CMS (1796–1873), views shared outside Europe by the director of the American Board of Foreign Commissioners, Rufus Anderson (1796–1880) and Karl Graul of the Leipzig Mission. For Gustav Warneck, the Pietist and Moravian stress on winning individuals to salvation had to be combined with planting churches and churches that were 'of the soil', sharing the culture, national character and life of indigenous people.

This kind of emphasis, as also the increasing cultural sensitivity of the missionary anthropologists to the cross-cultural element of missionary work and evangelization, was the most promising legacy of European missionary expansion towards the 20th century.

'Every period of mission leads to Christianization of the ethnic group... [it] begins with the conversion of individuals... the church in every nation conveys the native traits and characteristics of the whole ethnic life.'

G. WARNECK,
MISSIONSLEHRE

CHAPTER 7

Asia from 1500 to 1900

C hristian expansion into Asia after 1500, in sharp contrast to that achieved by the church of the East up to the time of Alopen, was heavily European, related to the expansion of the Portuguese and Spanish empires in the 16th and 17th centuries and to the Dutch, English, French and Danish trading interests in the 18th and 19th centuries. The Jesuits, and their 'Visitor to the East', Alessandro Valignano, and later the Propaganda Fidei under Francesco Ingoli (1578–1649), tried hard to detach Christian mission from the stranglehold put on it, for example, by the authorities in Lisbon, who tried to ensure that all missionaries and all correspondence on missions passed through their hands. In the later period, the relationship between the East India Company and its Dutch equivalent with missionary work was often to regard it as a threat to maintaining undisturbed relationships with the indigenous peoples on which trade could flourish. European trading and political weight, as in the time of the British 'Raj' in India (1857–1947), was by no means always advantageous to Christian mission.

Francis Xavier and Jesuit mission
Even before the Jesuit order had been finally recognized by Rome, its founder, Ignatius Loyola (1491–1556), became aware of the need for an able overseer of Asian missions. Reluctantly, and under pressure of circumstances, he sent his ablest lieutenant and close friend, Francis Xavier (1506–52), to Portuguese Goa in 1540. Xavier remains one of the greatest of all Christian missionaries, possessed it

Stained-glass
window
depicting Francis
Xavier. From the
cathedral of Ho
Chi Minh City,
Vietnam.

*'Many out here
fail to become
Christians
simply because
there is nobody
to make them
Christian. I have
[wanted] often
to go round the
universities
of Europe to
bludgeon those
people who have
more learning
than love...'*

FRANCIS XAVIER TO
IGNATIUS LOYOLA
IN A LETTER

seems of an immensely attractive personality and a Pauline determination to preach the gospel where it had not been named.

Xavier moved from Goa to the Parava (Bharathra) fishermen of the Coromandel coast of India, where he baptized thousands and was active in catechizing, though on his own account with a poor grasp of the language. He visited Sri Lanka (1541–45) and Indonesia (the Molucca

Alessandro Valignano (1539–1606)

Born into the Italian nobility, Valignano obtained a doctorate of law at the University of Padua. After a profound religious experience, he entered the Society of Jesus in 1566. He was appointed Visitor to the Eastern Missions in 1573. He sailed to Goa from Lisbon in 1574. A period of study in Macau led him to the influential decision that the Jesuit mission in China should concentrate on Chinese language, script and the understanding of Chinese custom and literature, a policy followed through by Michele Ruggieri and Matteo Ricci, the Jesuit pioneers of it. Valignano set his face against any conquistador approach to the high civilizations of China and Japan and set out his views in the work *Il Ceremeoniale per i Missionari del Giappone* of 1581, prepared with help from Japanese Christians. He paid two further visits to Japan in 1590–92 and 1598–1603. In China, Ricci, who studied Confucianism deeply enough to be accepted by the Chinese Confucian *literati*, both exemplified Valignano's policy and in his *Journal* regarded him as founder of the Catholic church in Japan of the time.

Islands) for two years before entering Japan in 1549. He established Jesuit missions in Japan and had two catechetical books translated into the language. Exposure to Japan, with its deep respect for all things Chinese, made him determined to enter China. He was poised to do so on the off-shore island of Shang-Chiuan when he died in 1552.

Although Xavier failed to enter China, Valignano, who

Detail of a 17th-century screen depicting Jesuit priests and Japanese women.

reached Japan in 1578, became equally convinced of its importance as a mission field and that neither Japan nor China were to be approached (as the Spaniards had approached the Philippines since Magellan made contact in 1521) as if by conquistadors. Instead, careful accommodation to their highly developed civilizations would be needed. This led Valignano, an Italian, to resist the introduction of missionary orders influenced by such a conquistador mentality from the Spanish and Portuguese possessions. Two remarkable Jesuits followed through this policy in imperial China.

Inroads into China

Matteo Ricci (1552–1610) and Michele Ruggieri (1543–1607) entered China in 1583. In due course, they and their successors were to earn the deep respect of the Chinese, not least for their mathematical and astronomical abilities. Ruggieri, a lawyer from Puglia in Italy, worked with Ricci in Portuguese Macau before moving to the mainland. Together, they produced a Portuguese–Chinese dictionary, and Ruggieri later composed the first Chinese Catholic catechism; he was sufficiently proficient in the language to write Chinese poetry. Ricci, an outstanding intellectual, mastered the Confucian classics and came to believe that the kind of grounding he had received in the works of Thomas Aquinas and his use of Aristotle was compatible with the moral ideals set out by Confucius. Ricci's work of 1603 *Tiangzhu Shiyi* (The Meaning of the Lord of Heaven) adopted this approach in reaching out to the Chinese intelligentsia. Ricci believed that participation by Christians in Chinese ancestor rites did not compromise their Christian belief.

From 1600 Ricci had been permitted to reside in Beijing. His successors, like Father Ferdinand Verbiest (1623–88) and Father Schall von Bell (1592–1666), also greatly admired, were given official positions by the first Q'ing emperor, Kangxi (1654–1722; emperor 1662–1722)

Opposite page: Portrait of a Chinese convert by Sir Godfrey Kneller.

*'In no way… can
Christians be
allowed to
preside… at
the solemn
sacrifices… at
the time of each
equinox to
Confucius and
other departed
ancestors.'*

POPE CLEMENT XI IN
A DECREE, 1704

and they were able to cast the mantle of their positions of honour to protect other missionaries. Schall von Bell, however, narrowly escaped execution in 1664 in an often volatile situation. It was a tragedy that, after the combined influence of Valignano's policy of accommodation had been followed through with such success by Ricci and his Jesuit companions, even Propaganda Fidei's defence of the policy was eventually overturned in Rome. The so-called Rites Controversy, which hinged on how far the honouring of ancestors was a civil or religious act,

**Engraving of
Matteo Ricci
(1522–1610)
with Li Paul.
Ricci made
outstanding
contributions to
mathematics,
astronomy and
linguistic
sciences.**

involving Christians in superstitious practice (at its height between 1693 and 1704), in which dispute Rome ruled against the kind of accommodationist position advanced by Ricci, alienated the good-will gained by the Jesuits and dissipated its effect, so that Christianity became viewed as foreign and a religion of foreigners. The issues raised by the rites dispute were not finally laid to rest until 1939, when Catholics were finally allowed to take part in ancestral veneration and the rites were accepted as civil demonstrations of honour, which had lost any earlier pagan associations.

India

In India another apostle of accommodation and a Jesuit, Robert de Nobili (1577–1656) had immersed himself in Hinduism, both its philosophy and its way of life. He, like Valignano an Italian by birth, intended to detach himself from strongly Portuguese and European models of Christianity. He succeeded in commending his form of Christian faith to Indians and became responsible for a number of high-caste Brahmins becoming Christians. His methods, however, raised controversy among his superiors and for a time he was forbidden to baptize.

Like Ricci in China, de Nobili in Madurai stood for great sensitivity towards the culture and life of the host country and suffered misunderstanding from co-religionists through their fears of compromise. Alexandre de Rhodes (1591–1660), a Jesuit pioneer in modern Vietnam, made himself persona non grata with the Portuguese for his firm advocacy of indigenous clergy, which they understood as a breach of the *padroado*. Missionary initiatives and deep identification with alternative language and culture were often met by disapproval from the authorities, political or religious. Despite problems with both Portuguese and Vietnamese authority, including de Rhodes's expulsion, by 1640 there were some 100,000 Christians as fruit of the Jesuit mission in Vietnam.

'Father Nobili said, "I too shall become an Indian to save the Indians"... he introduced himself to Brahmins... as a sannyasi i.e. a penitent who has renounced the world,'

THE JESUIT
PROVINCIAL'S
DESCRIPTION OF
DE NOBILI, 1609

Japan

Japan, too, after Xavier, enjoyed a period of great progress. Valignano, visiting in 1580, declared himself deeply impressed with the quality of Christian life to be found in Japan. By 1583 there were 200 churches and some 150,000 Christians. In one town south of Kyoto around 8,000 had been baptized in 1579. The Jesuit mission was well led by Francisco Cabral (1528–1609), a leader of Portuguese noble extraction, between 1570 and 1583. Ultimately, however, he and Valignano differed over the advance of the Japanese indigenous ministry (espoused as ever by Valignano) and Cabral left. There was a sharp change in the attitude of the political authorities later in the century and in 1614 there was an expulsion order on all Jesuits. Fierce persecution then followed on the 300,000 Japanese Christians (in a population of some 20 million). Christians were crucified in Nagasaki in 1597 and there were further mass executions in 1622. The policy was pursued with great savagery between 1627 and 1634 and resulted in many 'hidden Christians', whom 19th-century missionaries found had retained their knowledge of many of the symbols of the Christian faith, when Japan opened two centuries later after 1859. Despite the tragic outcome of their work, one recent authority from outside Roman Catholicism, Andrew Ross, has judged the Jesuit mission in Japan to have been the most successful approach to a sophisticated society of any since the conversion of the Roman empire.

'Do not attempt in any way to persuade these people to change their customs... what could be more absurd indeed than to transport France, Italy or some other European country to the Chinese?'

PROPAGANDA FIDEI
INSTRUCTION OF 1659

Protestants in Asia

From 1600 both Dutch and English trading interests became increasingly important in Asia, not least because of their nations' maritime superiority. The Dutch established themselves in Indonesia and created a centre at Batavia (Jakarta). Their trading company, Verenigde Oost-Indische Compagnie (VOC), founded in 1602, meant that Reformed religion reached the East Indies, though it did not conduct significant missionary work among indigenous peoples. Its English equivalent, the East India Company, founded in 1600, although highly suspicious of missionaries, appointed chaplains to their trading communities. This provided an opening for those with missionary vision in England and India such as William Wilberforce and Charles Grant, an employee of the company.

Two outstanding EIC chaplains were Henry Martyn (1781–1812) and Claudius Buchanan (1766–1815). Martyn had been one of the leading young Cambridge intellects of his day and was a winner of university prizes. He and other Cambridge men of his time had been influenced by the long ministry of Charles Simeon (1759–1836), with his preaching of the gospel for all peoples. Martyn proved a brilliant linguist and translator. He was appointed a chaplain in 1805, translated the New Testament into Urdu and Persian and prepared an Arabic version before his early death from tuberculosis aged 31. His Indian

The East India Company

The East India Company was the source of British influence in India until the Crown took direct responsibility after 1857. It was run by a court of directors in London. The company's main rivals in India were the French but it raised its own army under its employee Robert Clive (1725–74) and defeated them at Plassey in 1757, one of the decisive battles of world history, which led to the control of Bengal and British supremacy in India. For 100 years the company effectively ruled Bengal, though from 1784 British politicians created a system of dual control. Great fortunes were made by returning Englishmen, known as the 'nabobs', and there were accusations of peculation, most famously in the case of Warren Hastings (1732–1813). The 'Indian Mutiny' of 1857 led to government by the crown after 1858 until Indian independence in 1947.

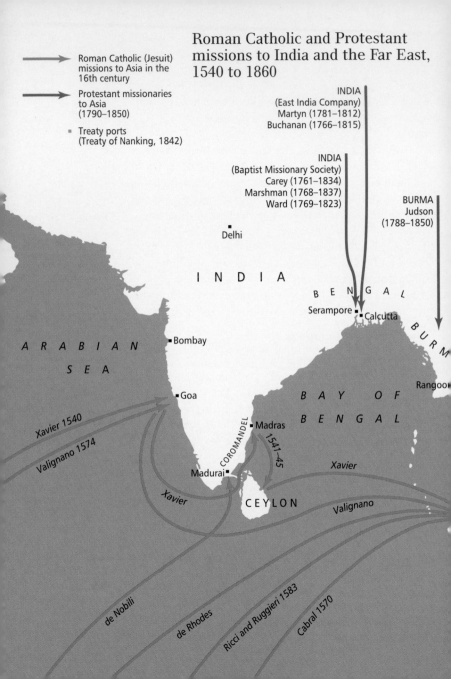

Roman Catholic and Protestant missions to India and the Far East, 1540 to 1860

→ Roman Catholic (Jesuit) missions to Asia in the 16th century

→ Protestant missionaries to Asia (1790–1850)

▪ Treaty ports (Treaty of Nanking, 1842)

INDIA
(East India Company)
Martyn (1781–1812)
Buchanan (1766–1815)

INDIA
(Baptist Missionary Society)
Carey (1761–1834)
Marshman (1768–1837)
Ward (1769–1823)

BURMA
Judson
(1788–1850)

Delhi

I N D I A

B E N G A L

Serampore — Calcutta

B U R M A

A R A B I A N
S E A

▪ Bombay

▪ Goa

Xavier 1540

Valignano 1574

Rangoo

B A Y   O F
B E N G A L

C
O
R
O
M
A
N
D
E
L

▪ Madras

1541–45

Xavier

Madurai ▪

Xavier

C E Y L O N

Valignano

de Nobili

de Rhodes

Ricci and Ruggieri 1583

Cabral 1570

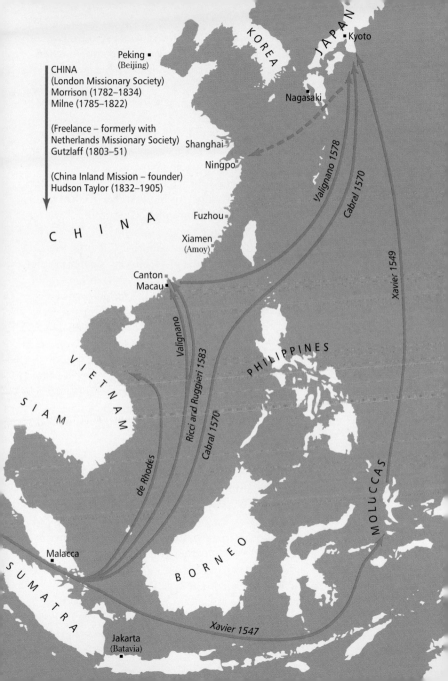

KOREA

JAPAN ■ Kyoto

■ Peking
(Beijing)

CHINA
(London Missionary Society)
Morrison (1782–1834)
Milne (1785–1822)

(Freelance – formerly with
Netherlands Missionary Society)
Gutzlaff (1803–51)

(China Inland Mission – founder)
Hudson Taylor (1832–1905)

Nagasaki ■

Shanghai ■

Ningpo ■

C H I N A

Fuzhou ■

Xiamen ■
(Amoy)

Canton ■
Macau ■

Valignano 1578

Cabral 1570

Xavier 1549

S I A M

V I E T N A M

Valignano

PHILIPPINES

Ricci and Ruggieri 1583

Cabral 1570

de Rhodes

■ Malacca

S U M A T R A

B O R N E O

M O L U C C A S

Xavier 1547

■ Jakarta
(Batavia)

assistant, Abdul Masih (1765–1827), converted from Islam to become a Christian missionary colleague and notable advocate of the faith, and was eventually ordained in 1825 as the first Indian Anglican clergyman. Others were inspired by Martyn's life of scholarship and devotion.

REV^D HENRY MARTYN. B.D
LATE
FELLOW OF ST JOHN'S COLLEGE, CAMBRIDGE.
and Chaplain to the Hon. E.I. Company.
AT BENGAL.

Engraving of
Henry Martyn
(1781–1812)
by W.T. Fry.

Claudius Buchanan was a Scotsman. Leading evangelicals arranged for him to attend the university of Cambridge; he joined other 'Sims', as Simeon's followers were called, in India, in particular David Brown, on his appointment as EIC chaplain. Buchanan served as vice-provost of Fort William College, Calcutta, founded by the Duke of Wellington's elder brother, Lord Wellesley, then governor general of India, and showed his missionary vision by endowing essay prizes on missionary subjects at the universities of Oxford and Cambridge, the Scottish universities and Trinity College, Dublin. In 1806 Buchanan was invited by the archbishop of Canterbury to become the first bishop in India but declined. A missionary-minded chaplain who did become a bishop and was also a 'Sim' was Daniel Corrie (1777–1837), the first Anglican bishop of Madras.

William Carey (1761–1834), who had been both a shoemaker and a Baptist preacher in Northamptonshire and is often regarded as the father of Protestant missions (though John Eliot, Ziegenbalg and others could be said to have a prior claim), arrived in India in 1793. He was soon joined by two other Baptist giants in Joshua Marshman (1768–1837) and William Ward (1769–1823), making up what became known as the 'Serampore trio', when they settled in the Danish possession. It is clear that they greatly admired the Moravians and tried to shape their own community life on Moravian models. Carey had been denied a passage by the EIC and his calling was derided by

'A nest of consecrated cobblers.'

SYDNEY SMITH,
EDINBURGH REVIEW,
APRIL 1809

critics like Sydney Smith, the satirical writer and clergyman who wrote for the *Edinburgh Review* at home.

Carey, however, by steady perseverance, not least in monumental labours at biblical translation, as well as in family tragedies and losses of precious manuscripts by fire, faced down all his critics, becoming in time Professor of Sanskrit at Fort William College and earning the accolade from Bishop Stephen Neill, himself a missionary in India: 'In the whole history of the church no nobler man has ever given himself to the service of the Redeemer.'

Scotland supplied a rich vein of missionaries in India after Buchanan. Alexander Duff (1806–78) won respect for his educational approach, with its equal measure of belief in the Bible and western science and literature as a means of reaching high-caste Indians. The Indian reformer, never a Christian, Ram Mohun Roy, respected and co-operated with Duff's efforts. Duff was to become the first professor of missions at New College, Edinburgh in 1866 after serving for 30 years in the field and declining the vice-chancellorship of the university of Calcutta.

Duff's service straddled the period when the EIC gave way to the Raj. Between 1857 and 1947 a number of outstanding Scottish missionaries and educators served in India, including John Wilson (1804–75), who became vice-chancellor of Bombay University; Alfred Hogg (1875–1954), principal of Madras Christian College and powerful analyst of Christian–Hindu issues; and another brilliant scholar and writer in John Nicol Farquhar (1881–1929), LMS missionary and finally professor of comparative religion at Manchester after 30 years' service in India.

For North Americans, an equivalent figure to Carey as a pioneer was the great missionary to Burma (Myanmar) Adoniram Judson (1788–1850). Judson had received missionary inspiration from reading sermons of Claudius Buchanan in 1809 and, after ordination as a Congregationalist minister, offered to the American Board of Commissioners for Foreign Missions in 1810. On the

'*What a treasure must await such characters as Paul and Elliot and Brainerd and others.*'

WILLIAM CAREY, *AN ENQUIRY INTO THE OBLIGATIONS OF CHRISTIANS TO USE MEANS FOR THE CONVERSION OF THE HEATHEN*, 1792

'*In the very act of acquiring English, the mind, in grasping new terms... ideas... must be tenfold less the child of pantheism, idolatry and superstition.*'

ALEXANDER DUFF, *INDIA AND INDIAN MISSIONS*, 1839

voyage out to India, he and his wife became convinced of
Baptist views. On arrival in India he was baptized, having
made his change of mind known to William Carey. He
was refused permission to work by the EIC as a Baptist
missionary in India but began work in Rangoon in 1813.
His work among the Karen people met with considerable
response. The first Karen baptized, Ko Tha Byu
(1778–1840), who came from a background of violent
crime, became a notable lay evangelist. The Karens
became the largest Christian group and in modern
Myanmar number some 200,000 Christians in over
1,000 churches. Judson himself became something of a
missionary icon and hero in mid-century North America.

China and Japan: fresh departures

China had effectively closed its doors to foreigners of all
kinds after imperial edicts against Christian preaching in
1720. Robert Morrison (1782–1834) was a lone Protestant
witness as LMS missionary from 1807, often at risk of his
life. Although the EIC proved hostile to his plans, from 1809
he accepted employment from them as an interpreter in
order to remain on Chinese soil. With the help of another
LMS missionary, William Milne (1785–1822), he translated
the whole Bible by 1819 and created a Chinese dictionary
between 1815 and 1823, which became a standard work. He
and Milne founded an Anglo-Chinese school in Malacca, of
which Milne was the first headteacher, followed by the
scholar, fellow Scot and LMS missionary, James Legge in
1840, who later became the first professor of Chinese at
Oxford in 1876.

All missionary incursion into wider China was
impossible, however, until the treaties of the mid-century
opened up the country by degrees. First, the so-called
'treaty ports' became accessible in 1842 (by the Treaty of
Nanking, a treaty forced on China by British commercial
interests, not least towards the import of opium from India
after the 'Opium Wars' of 1839–42); and the later treaty of
1858 (the Treaty of Tientsin), which opened the interior to

missionaries, preparing the way among other institutions for the China Inland Mission's penetration after 1865.

James Hudson Taylor (1832–1905) was born in Barnsley in Yorkshire to a devoutly Methodist family. He trained as a doctor, but, before he qualified, his offer of missionary service to the China Evangelization Society was accepted. Owing to the political conditions prevailing in China during the Taiping rebellion (read by some as a movement of Christian promise), he was sent to Shanghai (Guangzhou) in 1853. The Taiping rebellion was subsequently crushed by General 'Chinese' Gordon (later of Khartoum) in 1864. Taylor joined a missionary community in Shanghai, mostly LMS and CMS, profiting from the treaty of 1842. He claimed inspiration from Karl Gutzlaff (1803–51), who had travelled to the interior

Karl Gutzlaff (1803–51)

Gutzlaff was the son of a German tailor, who was educated at a Moravian school. He met Robert Morrison as a young man, which may have influenced him towards China. He offered to the Netherlands Missionary Society in 1824 and served initially in Siam (Thailand). He translated the Bible into Thai in three years. In 1828 he broke with NMS because they would not send him to China. He became a freelance missionary, distributing Christian literature along the coast. After Morrison's death he succeeded him as interpreter for the EIC in Guangzhou. He helped the EIC to negotiate the Treaty of Nanjing in 1842. He recruited various Chinese nationals as 'evangelists' to the interior and raised funds for their support through his writings in Europe, only to find that many of his recruits had deceived him and taken the money for other purposes. Although discredited in the eyes of some, Gutzlaff's probity was not in doubt nor his missionary zeal. Hudson Taylor looked on him as 'grandfather' of the CIM and its work in the interior provinces.

*'Prayed for
twenty-four
willing, skilful
labourers
at Brighton,
June 25, 1865.'*

NOTE ON THE
FLYLEAF OF HUDSON
TAYLOR'S BIBLE ON
THE BIRTH OF CIM

of China between 1833 and 1839 as a freelance missionary.

Taylor experimented with identification in Chinese dress and 'queue' (pigtail) on the advice of a veteran missionary in China, W.H. Medhurst (1796–1857), to the dismay of many other members of the missionary community. In 1857 he resigned from the CES. Deeply stirred by the needs of the unevangelized Chinese of the interior, he founded the China Inland Mission (CIM) in 1865, aiming to put two missionaries in each province, areas now open to foreigners after the Treaty of Tientsin of 1858. By now a fully qualified doctor and married to Maria Dyer, daughter of a missionary and a leader in her own right, he set out with a party of 16 from London to Shanghai on the *Lammermuir* in 1866, narrowly avoiding total loss by shipwreck.

From the beginning the CIM was to be a so-called 'faith mission', with no public appeals for funds; and its

**James Hudson
Taylor.**

missionaries accepted the absolute, if gently exercised, authority of Taylor himself, described by the American missionary W.A.P. Martin as the 'Loyola of Protestant missions'. In time, CIM numbered over 800 missionaries, including Methodists, Baptists, Anglicans and Presbyterians and others, and it planted churches that had a membership of some 80,000 by 1897. The profile of the society had been greatly enhanced in the 1880s by the advent of the so-called 'Cambridge Seven', two of whom were well-known sporting heroes at home and held to be making very great sacrifices. C.T. Studd (1860–1931) was one of these, later to be founder of World Evangelization Crusade (WEC) and the Heart of Africa Mission, which worked in the Belgian Congo. Hudson

Taylor's publication, *China's Millions*, achieved a circulation
of 50,000 at this time and also helped to put the mission in
front of the public. Although the society suffered heavily in
the Boxer Rebellion (1898–1900), when 200 missionaries,
many of them Roman Catholic, and around 30,000 Chinese
Christians lost their lives (CIM lost 58 missionaries and
some children out of a total Protestant loss of 130), the
society refused indemnities by policy. It continued to be an
influential Christian body under the second director, Dixon
Hoste (1861–1946), himself one of the Cambridge Seven,
but in 1949 all missionary personnel were expelled by
the Communist regime. Taylor himself was described by
Latourette as 'one of the four or five most influential
foreigners who came to China in the 19th century for any
purpose, religious or secular'.

Another influential figure, Timothy Richard
(1845–1919), originally applied to the CIM for service but

Timothy Richard,
seated at a desk
in his library
at Shanghai,
8 June 1909.

was finally sent by the Baptist Missionary Society in 1869 to work in Shandung province. His reputation as a leading Christian humanitarian grew after his outstanding relief work during the famine in the province and North China in 1876–79. He had been drawn at first by the evangelical biblicism of the CIM but he moved into a liberal theology, which caused him to dissociate from the BMS and to concentrate on literary and journalistic work, aiming to reach the Chinese intelligentsia, social leaders and the source of supply for the Chinese civil service. In 1891 he became director of the Christian Literature Society, which pursued these aims, based in Shanghai. He associated with leading Chinese reformers at the turn of the century and through them his ideas became widely influential. He adopted a more collective approach to reaching the Chinese nation with the gospel and was regarded with some suspicion by those like Hudson Taylor, who placed heavy emphasis on the salvation of individuals and the planting of congregations. He was also strongly affirmative of Chinese religion, especially Mahayana Buddhism, which to him had many affinities with Christian teaching. A controversial figure, with individual perceptions and conviction, he was one of the best known Christian leaders in China by 1900.

'Hidden Christians' in Japan

Japan had been closed to foreigners since the severe persecutions of Christians and the expulsion of the Jesuits in 1614. This policy had been pursued by the Tokugawa regime between then and the 19th century. A new government, known as Meiji Restoration, responded differently to political, commercial and missionary initiatives. The government of the USA used a naval squadron under Commodore Perry to re-open trading relations with foreigners in the 1850s. By a treaty of 1859 missionaries were able to take advantage of the new situation; the edict of 1612 against Christianity was finally officially repudiated in 1873. Meanwhile, American

Protestant missionaries, as well as Roman Catholic and Orthodox, discovered many 'hidden Christians', who had preserved certain forms of the faith since the 17th century.

They knew the Lord's Prayer, the Ten Commandments, the Hail Mary and the framework of the liturgical year; images of Buddha have come to light that, when reversed, reveal a crucifix. In addition to those at Nagasaki, one modern estimate has suggested 50–80,000 such Christians in island retreats on the Gotto Islands, where a lay organization consisted of various forms of responsibility such as 'father-leader' and 'teacher-baptizer'. Such groups were reluctant to re-join the Roman Catholic church, which had given them birth, for fear of losing their own developed life.

Meanwhile, between 1860 and 1900, the Orthodox church was given remarkable leadership in mission in Japan by Nicholas Kassatkin (1836–1912), who baptized his first Japanese converts in April 1868, built an Orthodox cathedral on land overlooking Tokyo in the 1870s, and by his death had commissioned 34 Japanese evangelists and organized the church into 260 congregations served by a largely indigenous ministry, which included 35 Japanese priests and a total membership of 33,000. American Episcopalians and other Anglicans, including Canadians, and Presbyterians and others, also developed missionary work.

Korea

Until 1865 Korea had been similarly closed to foreign influences, though there had been baptisms of Korean visitors to China in the 18th century, leading to an infant Roman Catholic church with a Chinese priest (owing entirely to Korean initiative); and some missionary involvement by members of the Société des Missions Étrangères de Paris in 1835. There was persecution over the issue of ancestor worship, which Christians were held to have abolished, and a number of executions. Even in the 1860s Christians were feared as a fifth column when

'There were two main leaders in most of the villages... the prayer leader... the baptizer [who] had to have with him a pupil baptizer to succeed him.'

PETITJEAN'S
DESCRIPTION OF THE
HIDDEN CHRISTIANS
OF NAGASAKI, 1865

Russian political pressure threatened and there were estimates of thousands of martyrs. The first Protestant missionary, R.J. Thomas of LMS, paid with his life when attempting to import Chinese Bibles. Despite many difficulties and helped by toleration of religion in the 1880s, there was a remarkable expansion of the church in Korea, due in some measure to the work of the Presbyterian missionary J.L. Nevius (1829–93). His 'Nevius Plan' capitalized on the same 'three self' formula – churches becoming self-supporting, self-governing and self-extending – that was so important to the mission administrators Henry Venn and Rufus Anderson. After 1900 Korean churches experienced revivals and these, combined with Japanese attempts to stamp out Korean national culture (resulting in wider and deeper adherence to the church), made for the immense Christian population of today, when 15 million Christians in over 200 denominations are to be found, mostly in South Korea, and over 10,000 are serving as missionaries.

Although this conclusion trespasses into the subject of the final chapter on the 20th century, it may be as well to summarize the shape of Asian Christianity today, much of which has resulted from European expansion since 1500. Indonesia is largely Muslim but has some 20 million Christians who make up 16 per cent of the population. Roman Catholic life is especially present in the Philippines, a Spanish colonial possession until 1898, when the USA assumed government for a time. Twenty-seven million people regard themselves as Roman Catholic and Christians make up 90 per cent of the population. At the other end of the scale, Japan remains largely impervious to Christian influence, although there have been Christians who have been prominent in public life and others, such as Toyohiko Kagawa (1888–1960), who have been internationally renowned Christian individuals. Christians, however, remain only one per cent of the population of 120 million. China presents a more puzzling picture, with details elusive from the Communist regime.

There seems little doubt that Chinese Christians run into millions. By 1900 there were half a million Roman Catholics and around 40,000 Protestants. An informed and authoritative source has suggested that Roman Catholics now number between 10 and 12 million and Protestants 15 million; in addition, there are large-scale syncretistic, or religiously mixed, movements which display some Christian practices and may number as many as 50 to 100 million more than those in traditional churches. India remains 80 per cent Hindu in religion, although formally a secular state; Christians are a mere two to three per cent of the remainder, though this figure may mean as many as 27 million Christians. So, Christianity in Asia has many millions of adherents, minorities in Japan and India, probable growth in China far exceeding 19th-century levels and strong populations of Christians in South Korea and the Philippines.

CHAPTER 8

Oceania

Captain Cook's voyages in the South Seas were one important way that Europe became aware of the islands of Polynesia, through his visit to Tahiti in 1769 and to New Zealand and Australia, some of the coastline of which he charted meticulously. Publications based on his journals fired the imagination of missionary-minded pioneers like John Williams (1796–1839), a Congregationalist minister and LMS missionary, who was commissioned to serve in Tahiti at the same time as Robert Moffatt was commissioned for South Africa by the LMS in 1816.

Tahiti

It was the LMS who provided the first pioneers earlier than this, when a party of 30 men, including four ordained ministers, sailed in the *Duff* in 1796. The rest of the party were so-called 'artisan missionaries' and the majority landed in Tahiti, though one went to Tongatabu in the Tongan group of islands and one to the Marquesas. This original party found their work sufficiently discouraging for most of the group on Tahiti to leave in 1798 to take refuge by ship to Sydney.

On Tahiti, the activities of a tribal chief became conclusive for the mission. Pomare II (1779–1821) had been forced to flee from the island, where he had befriended the missionaries and become literate through their teaching. While in exile on the island of Moorea, in company with the LMS missionary and bricklayer Henry Nott (1774–1844), Pomare was drawn increasingly to Christianity. When he returned to Tahiti and reasserted his authority in 1812 he declared for the Christian cause; and, after an attack on his life in 1815, he insisted on the destruction of idols

'Here the natives flocked around us in great numbers in as friendly a manner as we could wish, only that they showed a great inclination to pick our pockets.'

COOK ON HIS
ARRIVAL IN MATAVAI
BAY, TAHITI,
JOURNAL,
14 APRIL 1769

throughout the island, so paving the way for his own continued dominance and that of the Christian faith.

It was to this prepared situation on Tahiti that John Williams came aged 20. King Pomare became a baptized Christian in 1819, though his self-indulgent life left the missionaries dissatisfied. Williams, however, was not content to be restricted to Tahiti. He was eager to evangelize the other island groups and went first to Raiatea in the Windward Islands in 1818, where he formed a church in cooperation with the chief, Tamatoa; and, after

John Williams, killed by a native islander.

buying a ship, the *Endeavour*, reached out to more of Polynesia and then Melanesia. He worked on the island of Rarotonga between 1823 and 1833, pioneered Samoa using Polynesian Christians to assist him in visits of 1830 and 1832 and by 1834 was able to claim that no group or island of importance within 2,000 miles (3,200 kilometres) of Tahiti had been unreached. He returned to England to oversee the translation and printing of the Rarotongan New Testament (1834–38) but was back at work again in the Pacific in 1839, when he was attacked and killed on the island of Erromanga in the New Hebrides (Vanuatu) on 20 November 1839.

Australia and New Zealand

In 1788 the British government decided to use New South Wales as a convict colony and Botany Bay became their destination. William Wilberforce's Christian compassion extended to convicts as well as to slaves and he took a leading part in ensuring that the first convicts had the services of a chaplain. Richard Johnson, the chaplain, built the first church at his own expense and served until 1801.

Samuel Marsden (1764–1838) his successor was physically stronger, a Yorkshireman, product of the evangelical revival and of Magdalene College, Cambridge, where he had been strongly influenced, like the chaplains in India, by Charles Simeon. Marsden established himself as not only chaplain but also a successful sheep breeder and farmer at Parramatta and became a magistrate. It was Marsden who befriended the LMS missionaries when they arrived in Sydney in 1798 and in 1804 was made LMS agent for the South Seas. He encouraged the missionaries to persist in the period before Pomare's re-emergence as a Christian chief and befriended another party forced to flee in 1810. Marsden had also met and employed some Maori at Parramatta. In 1807 he urged the CMS to mount a mission to New Zealand. This project had to be put on hold after Maori plundered the ship *Boyd* and killed its crew, probably in revenge for European aggression, in 1809; but in 1814 Marsden was able to lead a CMS party with the help of a young Maori chief, Ruatara. The party was made up of two artisan missionaries in John King, a shoemaker, and William Hall, a carpenter, and a

Early missionary settlement in New Zealand at the Bay of Islands. Painting by Augustus Earle, 1827.

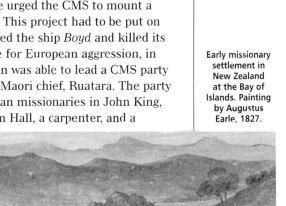

*'It being
Christmas Day
I preached from
the second
chapter of
St Luke's Gospel
and the 10th
verse, "Behold,
I bring you
glad tidings of
great joy."'*

SAMUEL MARSDEN
IN HIS JOURNAL OF
HIS VISIT TO NEW
ZEALAND OF 1814

*'All this is very
surprising when
it is considered
that five years
ago nothing
but the fern
flourished
here... the
lesson of the
missionary is
the enchanted
wand.'*

CHARLES DARWIN
ON THE CMS MISSION
IN NEW ZEALAND
IN 1835

schoolmaster, Thomas Kendall, who was ordained in 1820. Marsden preached the first Christian sermon on New Zealand soil on Christmas Day 1814, interpreted to his Maori hearers by Ruatara.

Between 1814 and his death Samuel Marsden, who was a bad sailor and suffered severely from sea sickness, made seven voyages to New Zealand and was regarded by the missionaries there (whatever his reputation as a 'flogging magistrate' in New South Wales) with the deep respect of a founding father and wise adviser to the mission. Both Methodist missions (with the friend of Marsden, Samuel Leigh, as pioneer) from 1822 and Marist (Roman Catholic) missions led by Bishop Pompallier, who arrived in 1838, were to share in the evangelization of the Maori.

After isolated baptisms in the 1820s, the Maori response was increasingly remarkable. According to William Williams, one of two notable brothers who were missionaries for CMS and a reliable witness, there were 30,000 Maori worshippers in CMS churches alone in the 1840s in the North Island. The first Anglican bishop of New Zealand, G.A. Selwyn, who arrived in 1841, by a strange mistake by clerks in London preparing his Letters Patent, was given authority over large areas of Melanesia. He capitalized on the error by engaging in missionary work in the Pacific himself and by recruiting a brilliant linguist in J.C. Patteson (1827–71) to extend the work in Melanesia, of which he was created Anglican bishop in 1861. Patteson was said to speak 20 Melanesian dialects. He established a school for boys from the islands on Norfolk Island in 1865, which aimed to produce an indigenous Melanesian ministry with a minimum of European impositions by way of cultural change in matters such as clothing.

Patteson, like John Williams, ultimately paid the price of martyrdom on the island of Nukapu in 1871, almost certainly a revenge killing for the kidnapping of five boys by 'blackbirders' shortly before his visit, taken to provide cheap labour for the plantations of Fiji or Queensland. Five wounds in his body and five fronds tied to it (held as a relic of martyrdom by the SPG) were evidence of this. Two notable Anglican priests continued Patteson's work on Norfolk Island: the first was his successor, R.H. Codrington (1830–1922), missionary and anthropologist, whose study *The Melanesians* (1891) remains important, along with his analysis of 'mana' (spiritual power) in such societies; and second C.E. Fox (1878–1977), who arrived on Norfolk Island in 1902 and earned great respect as priest among Melanesians and as a scholarly anthropologist.

Whereas the Maori were a people organized in settled communities, if warlike in character, the Australian aborigines represented quite a different challenge to missionary work. They were estimated to number some 300,000 prior to European contact and had lived in Australia for 20,000 years or more. The semi-mystical importance of the land to this nomadic people and due appreciation for their intricate culture has steadily escaped Europeans. As

The Revd Thomas Kendall with Maori chiefs Waikato (on the left) and Hongi Hika. Painting by James Barry, 1820.

*'Appalling and
inhuman
behaviour, which
can only be
called genocide,
characterized
settlement in
Tasmania.'*

IAN BREWARD,
AUSTRALIAN
PROFESSOR, IN HIS
HISTORY OF THE
CHURCHES, 2001

with the cases of native Americans and Canadians, their
treatment has been marked again and again by shameful
and exploitative episodes in colonial history. Tasmania
presented an extreme example of the general oppression
and lack of understanding. After racial clashes in the 1830s,
the aboriginal population of Tasmania was hunted down,
sometimes shot as prey, and finally transported to Flinders
Island, numbering then about 5,000 in 1835. Here,
separated from their land and ancient customs of their
ancestors, they became ultimately extinct in 1876.

There had been an early CMS mission to aborigines
in New South Wales in 1832, which gave up in 1843; and
a Methodist mission to Sydney's aborigines begun in 1821,
which also failed, though Methodism had some success
in Western Australia after 1840, as did Roman Catholic
Benedictines north of Perth after 1847. This mission
produced two candidates for the priesthood, who sadly
both died in Europe. Both Moravians and Lutherans in
Queensland tried to reach out to aborigines. By 1850, the
original population had been reduced to 10,000. European
diseases, including smallpox, typhoid, tuberculosis,
measles and influenza, to which they had no immunity,
contributed to a decline, in which cultural dislocation and
land disputes were also factors.

Polynesia and Melanesia
Of the three ethnic groups in the Pacific, Polynesian,
Melanesian and Micronesian, the Polynesians were both
the first to receive the Christian gospel and frequently
responsible for its extension to their own islands and those
of Melanesia also. If the islands of Hawaii and the special
case of Pitcairn are discounted, LMS had begun work in
islands like the Marquesas as far to the east of Australia
and New Zealand as any in the Pacific. For our purposes, a
treatment that works its way towards Australasia and the
great land mass of New Guinea from further east can make
for clarity. Tahiti, the original base for LMS missionaries,
was reinforced by men like William Ellis (1794–1872),

whose *Polynesian Researches* (1829) was probably second
only to Cook's journals in bringing life in the Pacific to a
wider public. Tahiti supplied John Williams with numbers
of Polynesian evangelists and teachers. It became a French
possession and in 1863 the LMS decided to hand their
work over to the Protestant Paris Mission (Société des
Missions Évangéliques de Paris).

Tahitian teachers had been established on Samoa by
Williams in the 1830s and LMS work there began in earnest
in 1836. The two sets of Samoan islands had a total
population of around 200,000 people and so constituted
a larger field than Tonga (50,000). In Tonga, however, the
Methodist WMMS (Wesleyan Methodist Missionary Society)
had remarkable success. Although Walter Lawry of their
mission had landed as early as 1822, it was Tahitian converts
like Hape, Tafu and Borabora who were effective between
1822 and 1827. Two important Europeans did arrive, John
Thomas (1796–1881) on Tongatabu, a blacksmith become
missionary who served from 1826–59, and Nathaniel Turner
(1793–1864) who already had experience of the Methodist
mission in New Zealand and arrived with three Maori
assistants in 1827. In Tonga, the breakthrough, as in so
many African cases, came with the conversion of the chief
Tupou (Taufa'ahau) in 1830, who took the name of King
George. In what became essentially a Methodist kingdom,
with 90 per cent Methodist adherence, one missionary,
Shirley Baker, was to resign his ministry to become prime
minister of the island kingdom and adviser to the king on
constitutional matters from 1860–90. Eventually, however,
he was judged a liability and deported by the British High
Commissioner. King George died in 1893 and Tonga became
a British protectorate after 1900.

Two Roman Catholic missionary orders were active
in the Pacific. One, the Marists (Society of Mary), already
mentioned here as in New Zealand, had its origin in the
missionary vision of Père Colin in France in 1815. It was
active in the Marquesas and in Futuna and Wallis Islands,
whose populations became entirely Roman Catholic. It

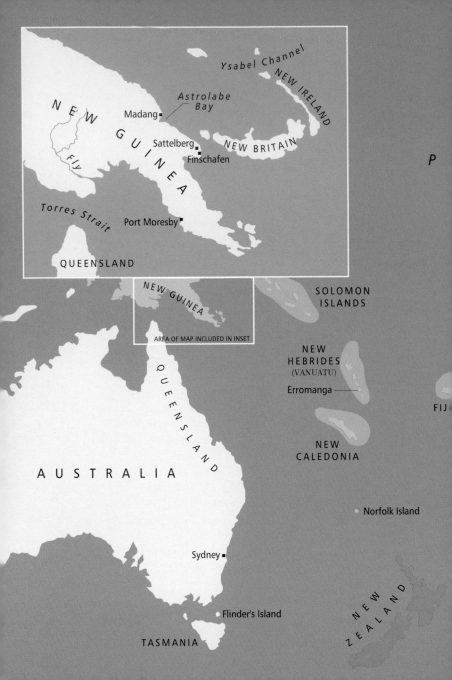

HAWAIIAN
ISLANDS
Hawaii
Molokai

Polynesia

Melanesia

P A C I F I C

O C E A N

MARQUESAS
ISLANDS

Wallis
Islands

SAMOA

utuna

Windward
Islands

SOUTHERN
COOK ISLANDS

SOCIETY
ISLANDS

TONGA

Raratonga

Tahiti

Tongatapu

Pitcairn
Island

Easter
Island

had its martyr in Father Pierre Chanel (1803–41), recruited for mission by Bishop Pompallier and a man described as serene and gentle in character, who was killed on Futuna after enduring much isolation and illness. He was canonized in 1954. The second order were the Picpus Fathers (the Congregation of the Sacred Heart of Jesus and Mary), confirmed as a missionary congregation by the pope in 1817 and given responsibilities in Oceania by the Propaganda in 1825.

Where the Marists were assigned western Oceania, the Picpus missions worked in islands like Easter Island and Hawaii. Here their most famous missionary was Father Damien (1840–89), Flemish in origin, who devoted himself to the lepers on the island colony of Molokai from 1873. He himself contracted the disease in the 1880s. By 1884 there were estimated to be 17,000 Roman Catholics on Hawaii. The pioneers there, however, had been the Protestant missionaries of the American Board of Commissioners for Foreign Missions. They had arrived in 1820, seen baptisms of the royal house in 1823 and by 1870 felt able to withdraw in the light of Christianization achieved, much of it through the assistance of Tahitian Christian chiefs and evangelists. Christian missions here, however, did not prevent a catastrophic decline in indigenous population: Polynesian numbers dropped from some 400,000 prior to European contact to 30,000 by 1900.

Space forbids attention to all the island churches and missions but Fiji (population 775,000), the Solomon Islands (368,000) and the New Hebrides, especially New Caledonia (200,000), deserve treatment before moving on to the larger land mass of New Guinea. The Solomon Islands have become a field of indigenous mission, not least through Anglican Melanesian missionaries, who have provided as many as 1,000 workers, a reminder that again and again in the Pacific it has been the initiative of native peoples that has been as influential as European missionaries. In recent times, the Melanesian Brotherhood, an Anglican order with simple vows, which

Gauguin and Tahiti

Paul Gauguin (1848–1903), the French artist who has left enduring images of Tahitian and Polynesian life on the European imagination, had worked in banking and finance in France. He abandoned this life for that of a painter. He reached Tahiti in 1891, where he produced a series of masterpieces that spoke of a vision of the 'noble savage' beloved of European philosophy but also of the sense of a Polynesian paradise lost. His work was not acclaimed in his own lifetime and he died heavily in debt. His work will now fetch millions in any currency.

Siesta by Paul Gauguin, 1894.

include a given number of celibate years for mission, have followed up the earlier initiatives of Bishop George Selwyn and Bishop Patteson, and of Bishop John Selwyn, son of the bishop of New Zealand. They built on the work done on Norfolk Island by Patteson, R.H. Codrington and C.E. Fox, himself the only European to be a member of the order. Methodists were active in the western Solomon Islands, and the Roman Catholic Father Epalle, first vicar apostolic for Micronesia and Melanesia, worked on the island of Ysabel, while the South Sea Evangelical Mission, with its remarkable founder, Florence Young, expanded its work among expatriate Melanesians and others in Queensland into the Solomons in 1904.

Fiji had an exceptional Tongan missionary in Joeli Bulu, who showed great awareness of the need to inculturate Christianity in Fijian forms, composing Fijian hymns and settings for the Lord's Prayer, the Creed and the Te Deum in Fijian chants, while also adapting their traditional funeral dirges to Christian use. John Hunt (1811–48), a Methodist missionary who arrived with Bulu in 1838, was equally and exceptionally sensitive to cultural issues in his decade of service. Again the breakthrough came with the conversion of the chief, Cakobau, who after early hostility, was greatly influenced by the conversion of his friend Varani through Hunt's ministry in 1845. Cakobau himself was finally baptized in 1854. Two years later there were some 30,000 church attenders and, even more significant, a social and cultural transformation in process, where the strangling of widows, polygamy and traditional cannibalism were steadily eradicated. Fiji became British in 1874. By 1914 there were around 80,000 Methodists and

Florence Young (1856–1940)

Born into a wealthy Plymouth Brethren family in Nelson, New Zealand, Florence Young began her work as a Sunday School teacher on their Queensland estate. This included working among Melanesian labourers. Some of these returned to their islands and formed Christian fellowships, who then appealed to Miss Young for teachers. She visited the Solomon Islands in 1904–1905 and founded the South Seas Evangelical Mission. She also served with CIM for some years in China. Today the SSEM, with some 63,000 members, is second only to the Anglicans in the number of Solomon Islanders who are members of its 600 congregations.

7,000 Roman Catholics, the results of Marist work from 1842 onwards. Methodists still predominate today, with around half of the population affiliated to them.

The New Hebrides and New Caledonia have special associations and famous names in their Christianization. The first, a largely Polynesian population with some Melanesians, contained the island of Erromanga, scene of John Williams's martyrdom in 1839. A total of six European missionaries lost their lives in this group of islands between 1839 and 1872. Samoan and Rarontongan missionaries were influential, beginning with the three Samoan Christians landed by Williams on Tanna. A very famous missionary, based on Tanna, was John G. Paton (1824–1907), a Church of Scotland minister who began work there in 1858. Paton's fame rested on his success in fundraising for the Pacific in tours of Australia, Canada and Britain and through his widely read autobiography. His fundraising paid for ships for missionary work, called successively *Dayspring*, and the fund continued to be the resource for five stations in the New Hebrides into the 20th century. Anglicans were also active after initial visits by G.A. Selwyn in 1848 and 1849; and Marists had some 1,000 baptisms and 3,000 catechumens by 1900. Politically the islands became a shared condominium between France and Britain from 1906.

New Caledonia became a French possession. Melanesian evangelists with connections to LMS had been pioneers here. The same combination of French government and LMS mission had been true of Vanuatu, where John Williams had planted some Samoan teachers in 1839. The French annexed the islands in 1853 and by 1900 there were some 11,000 Roman Catholics. The Paris Society (Protestant) had an outstanding missionary and anthropologist in Maurice Leenhardt (1878–1954), who joined the mission in 1897 and did notable missionary and anthropological work among the Kanaks. In company with R.H. Codrington, Leenhardt was among the foremost interpreters of the Melanesian world to the western

'God is not an import. He reveals himself.'

MAURICE
LEENHARDT

universities and became a professor of the Sorbonne and friend of Lévy Bruhl. He has been described as 'the greatest ethnologist among Pacific missionaries'.

New Guinea missions

Papua New Guinea, the eastern part of what in the west is part of Indonesia (Irian Jaya), with a population of 4 million people, was a major mission field. Once more, LMS were the early arrivals. In 1871, Samuel Macfarlane (1837–1911) established himself on Darney Island in the Torres Straits, which he hoped to turn into a kind of Iona for the mainland. He was joined by A.W. Murray (1811–92), another Scotsman from Jedburgh, who had served with the Samoan mission of LMS. W.G. Lawes (1839–1907), an even more influential figure, who had worked for LMS on the island of Niue, now became the first white man to live permanently on the mainland at Port Moresby in 1874, from which base he trained native Papuans to serve as missionaries. Lawes persuaded the British to create a protectorate, to defend Papuan rights against land-hungry Australians, in 1884 and he continued to press the administration towards guaranteeing Papuan rights thereafter. James Chalmers (1841–1901), another Scot and in his case a Congregationalist minister who had worked on Rarotonga for 10 years training Polynesians to be evangelists in New Guinea, joined the New Guinea mission himself in 1877. Like Lawes, he supported the British protectorate as a means of defence of Papuan rights. He became a friend of Robert Louis Stevenson and is said to have changed the writer's views of missionaries and their work. Chalmers was martyred by Papuan cannibals in 1901, while working to train Papuans and Polynesians for mission at Saguane on the Fly River. With him another 10 teachers and a young European missionary, Oliver Tomkins (uncle to an Anglican bishop of Bristol of the same name), were also murdered.

The courage involved in living among head-hunting tribes was not confined to these Scotsmen or the

'Here he lies where he longed to be; home is the sailor home from the sea and the hunter home from the hill.'

ROBERT LOUIS
STEVENSON'S
CHOSEN EPITAPH
FOR HIS GRAVE ON
SAMOA

Englishman, W.G. Lawes. In 1886 Johannes Flierl (1858–1947), of the German Lutheran Neuendettelsau mission, left work among the Australian aborigines for Finschafen, a station on one of the eastern tips of New Guinea. His work as a pioneer was followed by Christian Keysser (1877–1961), who earned a formidable reputation both as a missionary to the head-hunting Kate and Hube tribes and later as a writer and trainer of other missionaries in Germany; he had been refused renewed entry to New Guinea by the Australian authorities in 1920. Keysser, with his contemporary, Bruno Gutmann (1876–1966), who worked among the Chagga people of Kilimanjaro in Africa, pursued a corporate, tribal approach

Ludwig Nommensen (1834–1918)

North of New Guinea (Irian Jaya), in what in colonial days was Dutch Indonesia, lay the island of Sumatra. This was the home of the Batak tribe. In 1862, a remarkable missionary figure, native of Schleswig Holstein and member of the Rhenish Society, began work among the tribe. Over the years, Nommensen increasingly adopted a tribal approach to this people, and he was willing to emphasize the importance of *adat*, or tribal law and custom, in their life, and the traditional structure of elders in the church's development. Nommensen lost a child six years after his arrival and another four years later, before his wife died in 1887. Although he married again in 1901, another child was murdered in Sumatra in the same year, and his second wife died in 1909. Despite these personal tragedies, Nommensen gave 54 years of service to the Bataks. Initial baptisms had been made in 1865, a translation of the New Testament in the language was published in 1878, and a constitution was drawn up in 1881, which laid stress on the formation of a 'people's church', with Batak leadership and structure. The development of the work was helped by Dutch government generosity in grants towards education; many of the teachers supported were also Christian catechists. By Nommensen's death, the Batak church had 34 Batak pastors, serving in 500 local churches and supported by over 700 Batak teachers. Total membership had reached 180,000. Nommensen must be reckoned as one of the most outstanding missionaries in Protestant mission history.

Catholics of Enga province, Papua New Guinea, carry a huge wooden cross on a 250-mile journey from the village of Kandep to Mount Hagan in the Central Highlands.

'The folk church or tribal church is the goal of mission endeavour as pursued by the Lutherans.'

CHRISTIAN KEYSSER,
A PEOPLE REBORN

to mission work, which was widely studied. Keysser's attractively written books *A People Reborn* (German: *Eine Papuagemeinde*) and *Anutu im Papuagemeinde* (*Anutu* being the word the missionaries used for God) written in the 1920s popularized this so-called 'folk-mission' approach in Germany. As well as Finschafen, this German mission had a base in Sattelberg, while another German mission established itself in Astrolabe Bay in 1887. By 1910 the mission launched by Johannes Flierl had some 2000 baptized members and 13 different stations.

Of the other denominations in this large field, Methodists worked from the islands off the north-east coast from 1875; Anglicans established a mission on that coast in 1890, led by a Scottish Anglican priest, A.A. Maclaren, who died soon after his arrival. Roman Catholics entered New Guinea in 1889, led by Bishop Henri Verjus (1860–92) of the Sacred Heart Mission. His early death aged 32 did not prevent the mission receiving thousands of converts in its 25 churches. Roman Catholic work was strengthened by the arrival of SVD (the Society of the Divine Word) missions in New Guinea in 1895. This work was led by a German, Eberhard Limbrock (1859–1931), who had experience of China and whose exceptional leadership resulted in an integrated approach that included schools, cattle raising, bridge and road construction, saw mills, and docks and cargo ships as a way of improving the life of the people while advancing the mission's aims. The SVD had a reputation for respecting local culture and custom, a reputation shared by the Protestants of the Neuendettelsau mission; both missions produced works of value on ethnology and culture. By the time of Limbrock's death the SVD mission had some 20,000 Christians and another 5,000 under instruction.

Pitcairn Island, lying as far east of New Guinea as any Pacific island, is a special historical case. In 1789, the crew of the *Bounty*, a British ship commanded by Captain Bligh under instructions to visit Tahiti, mutinied against their captain. Bligh and the crew loyal to him were put in an open boat in which, by astonishing seamanship, Bligh crossed the Pacific to landfall. The leading mutineer, Fletcher Christian, realized that to stay on Tahiti invited recapture (Bligh did indeed return in 1792) but he had knowledge from charts of the existence of Pitcairn, to which he, with some crew and Tahitian men and women, resorted. It became a community riven by disagreements and violence before the surviving mutineers, with the aid of a Prayer Book and Bible, created a form of Christian life. In the 1890s, after a visit from a missionary ship, the community embraced Seventh Day Adventism, a denomination that has gained considerable strength in the Pacific since. Pitcairn, with its tiny population, has been administered from New Zealand as a British possession.

Cargo cults

One result of Christian mission in Oceania has been the emergence of so-called 'cargo cults' or, as they are now better known, adjustment movements. Typically these combined some Christian teaching with promises to cult members of European goods and bounty in the future. An early example was the new religion created by a Polynesian religious leader called Siovili in Samoa in the 1830s, with probable influence also on Tahiti. There was another such movement in Fiji in the 1870s. In the 20th century, cargo cults were important religious phenomena among the Melanesians of Papua New Guinea. In certain respects, the kind of missionary emphasis on material improvements noted above strengthened this connection between religion and expected material rewards. The Solomon Islands also developed such cults, examples of invigorating traditional religious ideas with a culturally adapted Christianity, sometimes in the face of misunderstandings by British, French or Australian representatives of government in their various territories.

In New Zealand, a succession of such Maori-inspired reinterpretations of religion occurred, 'Papahurihia' in the 1830s being the earliest, and 'Pai Marire' in the 1850–70 period being another. This latter movement was led by an ex-slave, Te Va Hamene, and mixed traditional practices with the biblical, so that an angelic expulsion of Europeans would lead to a Maori Canaan. Known sometimes as 'Hau Hau', the movement was held responsible for the death of the missionary Carl Volkner at Opotiki in 1865, but it now seems more likely that he had passed information to the British during the Maori wars and paid the penalty when this was discovered. 'Ringatu', which took on some aspects of the Hau Hau movement but also emphasized the Old Testament and Christian inheritance more heavily, developed in the 1860s and survives as a form of Maori church today.

Missionary impact

There has been a strand of European literature that has laid emphasis on the tragic consequences of Western contact in Oceania and Australasia and in some cases held the missionary movement responsible. The occurrence of the adjective 'fatal' in the title of a number of such studies has signified the corrupting influence discerned. There is no escaping the fact that Europeans introduced diseases to which the peoples of the Pacific had little or no resistance; populations were often decimated. It has to be remembered that crews of whalers, of sealing vessels and other European and North American incursions would have taken place with or without the missionaries' presence. The evils of prostitution, exploitative trading and kidnapping to staff the plantations were introduced independently of missionaries. Often, as has been shown, it was missionary intervention that prevented further exploitation by land-hungry colonialists in Australia, New Zealand and Papua New Guinea. Some evils can be traced back to missionary involvement. For example, the blankets with which the missionaries traded for food with the Maori were less healthy than traditional clothing – when damp and worn continually they were a probable cause of Maori susceptibility to deadly tuberculosis and influenza in the 1830s. By and large, however, missionaries were more often the protectors of the exploited than the sources of their decline.

Finally, it is important, as in the case of Africa, to underline how much of the expansion of Christianity in the Pacific was achieved by Polynesians, Melanesians and Micronesians themselves. We have noted Tahitian evangelists on Hawaii and on Tongatabu; a gifted and influential Tongan on Fiji; and Polynesians of different origins in many other island settings. Melanesians formed one highly effective indigenous agency in the Melanesian Brotherhood, with its 1,000 indigenous workers. There were well-authenticated examples in New Zealand of European missionaries finding worshipping communities of Christian Maori with no direct European contact, evangelism and teaching having been effected by Maori converts from other areas. Spontaneous expansion was an important part of the Pacific Christian experience.

'[In] the Pacific Islands... the people gave to the churches a larger place in their life than did the people of any other region.'

CHARLES FORMAN,
ISLAND CHURCHES OF THE PACIFIC

CHAPTER 9

The 20th Century: An African Century

In a history of Christian expansion, the 20th century must be dominated by the extraordinary development in sub-Saharan Africa, to which much of this chapter will be devoted. The contrast in Christian life and vitality can be made between the World Missionary Conference of 1910 in Edinburgh, where the historian of this immensely influential Protestant gathering noticed just one African from Liberia among a number of representatives from the younger churches of Asia; and the African Synod of Rome in 1994, with some 200 Africans including cardinals, archbishops and bishops as well as priests. The same point can be made about African Protestant leadership in the period after 1950, when men like Archbishop Erica Sabiti and Janani Luwum, who will appear later in this chapter, led the Anglican Church of Uganda in the 1960s and 1970s in parallel with a Roman Catholic leader like Cardinal Laurean Rugambwa, who attended the Second Vatican Council of 1963–65. In terms of wider statistics, 10 million African Christians (mostly from Egypt and Ethiopia) in 1900 became, by David Barrett's latest calculations, 335 million in 2000. Of these, some 83 million are estimated to belong to African Independent (sometimes African Initiated) Churches. These comprised 2,000 different denominations in 1968 and are well over 10,000 today. Some attempt, however inadequate, must be made to describe this extraordinary African Christian phenomenon in all its variety.

In an earlier chapter, the beginnings of 'Ethiopianism' and 'Zionism' were described, in particular the breakaway Ethiopian church founded by Mangena Mokone and recognized by Paul Kruger in the Transvaal as 'the Ethiopian Church of South Africa', which asserted an African expression of Christianity over against colonial and missionary-directed expressions. Zionism can be traced back to Zululand and a missionary, P.L. le Roux, who resigned from the Dutch Reformed Church in 1903 and called his Zulu congregation the Zionist Apostolic Church. After 1906 this became African-led and by 1930 there were Zionist congregations in Swaziland, the Transvaal and Rhodesia as well as in Zululand, laying emphasis on healing, speaking in tongues and extended times of worship. In the early years of the century, this African Christian consciousness was also experienced through a series of Christian 'prophets', religious revivalists to whom thousands of Africans responded by

Next pages:
A group of men dance at a meeting of the Zion Christian Church.

Zion Christian Church pilgrimage to Moria.

casting away and burning their fetishes and welcoming
baptism, often also reinforcing the mainline denominations
but sometimes resulting in breakaway churches.

African prophets and revival

Perhaps the most influential of all the prophets was
William Wade Harris (c. 1865–1929). Harris was born in
Liberia and a Methodist in background, though he was
later confirmed into the Protestant Episcopal Church
in Liberia. He was imprisoned in 1910 after a rebellion
against the Liberian authorities by his people, the Grebo.
While in prison he experienced a personal call to itinerant
preaching. He wore a white robe and a turban and carried
a baptismal bowl and a calabash rattle, travelling barefoot
with a cross-shaped staff and a Bible. The response to his
preaching over the border of Liberia in the Ivory Coast
was astonishing – it is estimated that it resulted in 100,000
converts in 1913. He also had a considerable impact in the
Gold Coast (now Ghana).

*'God is all
powerful, so you
must burn your
fetishes and love
one another.
Bring your idols
so that I can
burn them...
thereupon
I am going to
baptize you.'*

PREACHING OF
PROPHET HARRIS

Mainline denominations profited. Roman Catholic
baptisms, previously running at about 80 a year became
6,000 in 1915. The Methodist missionary, W.J. Platt, was
faced with 25,000 catechumens as a result of Harris's
campaigns when working in the 1920s. In addition, Harrist
churches developed throughout West Africa in countries
such as Ghana, Togo, Benin, Liberia and the Ivory Coast.
These were led by Harris's designated successor, E.J. (John)
Ahui (c. 1888–1992), who was styled 'Supreme Prophet of
the Harrist Church of West Africa'. Over 300 congregations
with 200,000 adherents made up this new denomination.
Harris's extraordinary effectiveness as a Christian
revivalist was recognized by the more traditional churches,
even if, as with others of the African prophets, there were
aspects of his teaching to which they could not subscribe,
notably his tolerance (and practice) of polygamy.

Garrick Braide (1880–1918) was a similar figure, who
originated in the Niger Delta area. He has been called the
first major Nigerian independent Christian prophet. Like

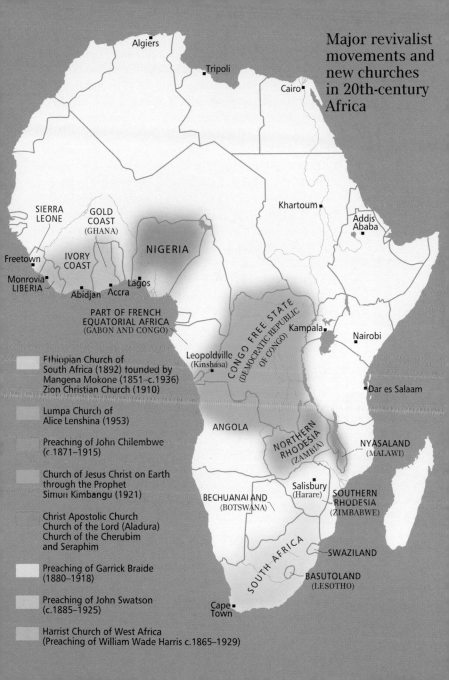

Major revivalist
movements and
new churches
in 20th-century
Africa

Algiers

Tripoli

Cairo

Khartoum

Addis
Ababa

SIERRA
LEONE

GOLD
COAST
(GHANA)

NIGERIA

Freetown

IVORY
COAST

Monrovia
LIBERIA

Abidjan   Accra

Lagos

PART OF FRENCH
EQUATORIAL AFRICA
(GABON AND CONGO)

Kampala

Nairobi

Leopoldville
(Kinshasa)

Congo Free State
(Democratic Republic
of Congo)

Dar es Salaam

Ethiopian Church of
South Africa (1892) founded by
Mangena Mokone (1851–c.1936)
Zion Christian Church (1910)

Lumpa Church of
Alice Lenshina (1953)

Preaching of John Chilembwe
(c.1871–1915)

Church of Jesus Christ on Earth
through the Prophet
Simon Kimbangu (1921)

Christ Apostolic Church
Church of the Lord (Aladura)
Church of the Cherubim
and Seraphim

Preaching of Garrick Braide
(1880–1918)

Preaching of John Swatson
(c.1885–1925)

Harrist Church of West Africa
(Preaching of William Wade Harris c.1865–1929)

ANGOLA

NORTHERN
RHODESIA
(ZAMBIA)

NYASALAND
(MALAWI)

BECHUANALAND
(BOTSWANA)

Salisbury
(Harare)

SOUTHERN
RHODESIA
(ZIMBABWE)

SOUTH AFRICA

SWAZILAND

BASUTOLAND
(LESOTHO)

Cape
Town

Harris he led a revivalist movement in 1915, which featured
opposition to traditional religion and mass baptisms. He
experienced imprisonment and religious resistance from
Anglicans; like Harris he was tolerant of polygamy. Nigeria
was also the scene of the development among the Yoruba
people of the Aladura groups (literally, 'praying people'),
which began as a response to the influenza epidemic
of 1918 and the search for healing. Three main Aladura
churches developed, the first of which, the Christ Apostolic
Church, owed much to Isaac Akinyele, brother to an
Anglican bishop, who became its president in 1941. A
second, which broke away to form the Church of the Lord
(Aladura), was led by Josiah Oshitelu, a baptized Anglican
and revivalist, who, in contrast to the first church, upheld
polygamy. The third was the Church of the Cherubim and
Seraphim, today a church of 4,000 congregations. One
informed observer, who is both a bishop and a university
lecturer, has judged that the future of the church in Nigeria
lies with these Aladura churches and that far from being
marginal they are now a central Christian reality in Nigeria.

In Ghana, a similar figure to Harris was John Swatson
(c. 1885–1925). Diplomatic handling of the revival movement
that he instigated resulted in many accessions to the
Anglican church during 1915–16. In Malawi, by contrast,
a tragedy unfolded in connection with the work of John
Chilembwe (c. 1871–1915). Between 1900 and 1914 this
Baptist leader, trained in Virginia, pursued quiet missionary
work in Malawi; but his following became radicalized by
colonial injustice, a sense of grievance exacerbated by African
conscription for the 1914–18 war. Violent insurrection
followed, in which Chilembwe lost his life and, by a strange
irony, a grandson of the great David Livingstone, who was
a farm manager of a large European estate where working
practices were felt to be oppressive, was decapitated.

The Congo and Kimbanguism

The Congo, with its very special history of European
administration as a prime example of the so-called

'scramble for Africa' by the European powers in the 19th century, also provided a special case of African Church Independency. King Leopold II of the Belgians had effectively owned vast tracts of central Africa as a private fiefdom or estate, administered through his own agents, one of whom was H.M. Stanley. The determined policy here was to make profits from rubber and ivory. On rubber collection, quotas were set to villages and savage punishments meted out where these were not met. This inhumanity provided Joseph Conrad, who visited the Congo, with the background to his novel *The Heart of Darkness*, set in the country. After a campaign mounted largely by a gifted journalist, E.D. Morel, who was able to use first-hand accounts of atrocities given to him by Baptist missionaries, the British consul Roger Casement was asked to report on the situation. He produced a document that caused a sensation in Europe and in 1908 led to the Belgian government taking responsibility for the territory.

Ten years later, an African of no formal education, Simon Kimbangu (c. 1889–1951), received what he believed to be a calling from Christ towards the conversion of fellow Africans, a calling that, like Jonah, he refused, and to escape which he fled to Kinshasha. In 1921, however, he began a ministry of healing in N'Kamba (his birthplace), which turned into a mass movement of revival. Like Harris, he preached against fetishes with a simple message of repentance and faith in Christ. Unlike Harris, he stood for monogamy. Within a few months of the mission of healing in April 1921 the authorities took fright, arrested him and sentenced him to death, a sentence commuted to life imprisonment by King Leopold. For 30 years (1921–51) he remained in prison but the movement grew rapidly. In time, L'Église de Jésus Christ sur la terre par le prophète Simon Kimbangu (The Church of Jesus Christ on Earth through the Prophet Simon Kimbangu) became one of the main denominations recognized by the authorities and in 1959, the year of recognition, had 1 million members. Joseph

'Nowhere else was there so systematic or long-standing a regime of oppression as in Leopold's Congo.'

ADRIAN HASTINGS,
*THE CHURCH IN
AFRICA*

Dagienda, Kimbangu's youngest son, was its leader and it became a member church of the World Council of Churches in 1969. Today it has 14,000 congregations, though its treatment of Simon Kimbangu as a virtual messiah has raised questions about the version of faith in Christ that it represents. Nevertheless, it is an extreme case of an African Independent Church growing from one imprisoned leader to its present position of a major denomination, accorded international recognition, with a membership of 7 million.

Growth and African leadership

There is a danger in a description of African Christian life such as the Kimbangu church for observers to neglect equivalent growth (and equivalent African leadership) in the more traditional churches. Uganda, with its strong response to Christianity since 1890, was an example where the two main traditional denominations, Roman Catholic and Anglican, benefited to the extent of millions of new adherents, so that today, of 19 million Ugandan Christians, 17 million may be regarded as either Roman Catholic or of the Church of Uganda (Anglican). The 20th century saw at least one outstanding African leader in each church. For Roman Catholics, Yohana Kitagana, in an almost Franciscan renunciation, forsook his assured position as a chief in 1901, gave away his property and became a missionary with staff and rosary in unevangelized areas of the country like the mountains of Kigezi. Among Anglicans, Apolo Kivebulaya (d. 1933), was ordained priest in 1903 and became a missionary to the pygmy people of the Congo around Mboga, where he died after 30 years of service. He laid the foundations of an entire Anglican province. Here were two African 'apostles', very different from Harris and Braide, also deeply committed to their calling, whose ministries resulted in growth and development in their traditional churches.

Uganda was also a country touched by a movement of

'Jesus Christ appeared to me in a dream on the night when I was doubting if I could endure being bound and prodded with spears and my house being burnt.'

APOLO KIVEBULAYA
ON HIS WORK AMONG
THE PYGMIES OF
MBOGA

Janani Luwum (d. 1977)

Luwum was one of the Ugandan Christians influenced by the
East African revival. He was ordained into the Anglican Church
of Uganda and became provincial secretary in the 1960s and
bishop of Northern Uganda in 1969. In 1977 he succeeded
Erica Sabiti, the first African
archbishop, who had followed
the Englishman, Leslie Brown.
In 1971 General Amin,
a British-trained soldier,
supplanted President Obote
while the head of state was at
a Commonwealth conference
in Singapore. His years of
power (1971–79) were years
of terror. Luwum and his fellow
Anglican bishops, as critics of the regime, incurred Amin's
enmity and vengeance. After arrest, Luwum was put to death
in 1977 by Amin's henchmen. Sabiti preached at his funeral
service outside Namirembe Cathedral in Kampala. Amin was
finally defeated by the Tanzanian army and exiled. Luwum is
commemorated in a chapel dedicated to 20th-century martyrs
in Canterbury Cathedral and in stone carvings to them on the
west front of Westminster Abbey unveiled in 1998.

**Archbishop
Janani Luwum
with Idi Amin.**

revival, which had profound effects in Ruanda and East
Africa in the 1930s. It originated in a deeply shared
European–African experience of personal renewal
between an English doctor, who was a CMS missionary,
J.E. (Joe) Church, and a Ugandan (Ganda) Christian,
Simeon Nsimbambi, which spread among the orderlies
at the hospital in Ruanda where Church was working.
Great emphasis was placed by the *balokole* ('saved ones')
on forgiveness through the saving blood of Christ,
on personal confession of sin and testimony to
personal salvation. The movement had its own hymn

'Tukutendereza Yezu'('We Praise You, Jesus, Jesus the Lamb'), and it mounted powerful Christian conventions. Many of the African leaders in East Africa, such as Archbishop Erica Sabiti and his successor, Janani Luwum, a martyr in General Amin's Uganda in 1977, Luwum's episcopal colleague, Festo Kivengere, and the Kenyan bishop of Fort Hall (Murang'a), Obadiah Kariuki, were deeply influenced by the revival. Kenya was the area where the depth of Christian life among the revival brethren was most severely tested and most impressively displayed. In the Mau Mau insurrection among the Kikuyu people of Kenya, taking the Mau Mau oath meant drinking blood and committing acts of violence. Those Kikuyu, Embu and Meru Christians who, when faced by intimidation and death, refused were in many cases *balokole* Christians. In at least one known instance, the reply was given 'I have drunk the blood of Jesus Christ and I can drink no other', to which the response was a blow intended to kill. While the East African revival had been potentially schismatic in the Church of Uganda, the stories of the Kikuyu martyrs showed the Christian depth and constancy of many of those it had reached.

Post-colonialism

After 1950, Africa entered a period of post-colonialism, as the European powers granted independence to one colony after another.

'The wind of change is blowing throughout the continent.'

HAROLD
MACMILLAN, BRITISH
PRIME MINISTER, TO
THE SOUTH AFRICAN
PARLIAMENT IN
CAPE TOWN,
JANUARY 1960

In 1952, President Nkrumah took power in the Gold Coast (Ghana), the first post-colonial African head of state. Independence and African leadership followed in Nigeria (1960), the Belgian colonies of the Congo, Ruanda and Burundi in the 1960s and the British colonies of Tanzania (1961), Kenya (1963), Malawi and Zambia (1964). The Portuguese territories of Angola and Mozambique followed in the 1970s. The leaders of these new nations had often been educated in mission schools; and in one case, Kenneth Kaunda of Zambia, the president was the son of a Presbyterian minister. Kaunda was faced with a

Christian movement resulting from a 'death and
resurrection' experience of a prophet, Alice Lenshina
(c. 1925–78), in 1953. Once more, a movement began that
aimed at the destruction of the fetishes of traditional
religion, acting also against witchcraft, polygamy, beer-
drinking and paganism. Alice Lenshina composed hymns
and many previously Roman Catholic or Presbyterian
church members joined the fold. Sadly, this 'Lumpa'
church movement confronted the new government of
independence with violence in 1964, over such issues as
the spread of schools, and as many as 1,000 people died,
Lenshina herself being imprisoned.

*'You who loved
the land of
darkness, let us
break through,
be saved. He will
help us in
everything, he
will take us out
of evil, when,
when?'*

TRANSLATION OF
BEMBA HYMN
COMPOSED BY ALICE
LENSHINA OF THE
LUMPA CHURCH

Apartheid and South Africa

This is not the place to pursue the history of the struggle
against the policy of apartheid in South Africa in detail,
but determined opposition of the policy by such figures
as Dr Beyers Naudé of the Dutch Reformed Church,
Trevor Huddleston of the Anglican Community of
the Resurrection at Rosettenville and Desmond Tutu,
a product of the seminary at Rosettenville and protégé
of Huddleston, achieved much towards deeper
Christianization in southern Africa. The Nationalist party
of Malan and Verwoerd had come to power in 1948 with
'separate development' as their aim, leading to the closure
of mixed race institutions founded by the churches at
centres like Lovedale. The policy was ruthlessly enforced
by the police, for example in the shooting of African
civilians at Sharpeville in 1960. Nelson Mandela's release
after 27 years in jail in 1990 marked the end of a searing
political struggle.

Desmond Tutu, appointed as Anglican archbishop of
Cape Town in 1986, was given the task of presiding over a
Truth and Reconciliation Commission (National Initiative
for Reconciliation) in 1990, which attempted to heal the
wounds inflicted during the struggle and which included
a confession from the Dutch Reformed Church that
apartheid was a sin.

Trevor Huddleston (1913–98)

Huddleston was an Anglican priest and member of the Community of the Resurrection, Mirfield. In 1963 he was appointed to lead the Anglican mission in Sophiatown, Johannesburg, known as the Church of Christ the King. He became one of the leading Christian campaigners against the policy of separate development adopted by the government. In 1956 he published the book *Naught for Your Comfort,* a widely read work on the South African struggle, which was critical of the government in South Africa and after which he was not permitted to return to the country. He became Anglican bishop of Masasi (Tanzania) in 1960. The young Desmond Tutu had known and admired Huddleston, who was a friend also of Nelson Mandela and Oliver Tambo. In 1968 Huddleston made way for an African successor in Masasi. He became in turn bishop of Stepney (1968–78) and archbishop of the Indian Ocean and bishop of Mauritius (1978–83) before retiring to Mirfield. From 1981 he was president of the Anti-Apartheid Movement.

Trevor Huddleston, renowned for his work in South Africa, addresses the press in London, 1956.

Threats to Africa's future

For the missionaries of the 19th century, the Christian expansion in Africa of the 20th century would have been difficult to believe, deeply committed as they were to their task. Nevertheless, not all of the scene would be so cheering, albeit in a widely Christianized Africa. Since the early 1980s, Africa has developed a HIV/AIDS pandemic, whereby an estimated 33 per cent of the population aged 15–49 years are infected, a situation that could have catastrophic effects on both the demographic and economic future of the countries. There are gleams of hope, for instance, in the falling infection rates in Uganda, but Africa faces a tragic crisis through the disease.

Secondly, it has been profoundly disturbing to many that areas such as Ruanda and Burundi, with a 90 per cent nominally Christian population, can be the context of ethnic violence of frightening savagery. The rivalry between the ruling Tutsi clan and the Hutu in Ruanda boiled over into the slaughter of 800,000 Tutsi by Hutu extremists in 1994 during three months. Twenty years earlier, in 1973, 100,000 Hutu had been treated similarly by the Tutsi. It is this kind of phenomenon that has caused sympathetic commentators like Adrian Hastings and Bishop Sundkler to view the massive accession to the historic churches and the independents as 'terrifying'; for the issue is whether such great numbers can be rooted, taught and nurtured, so that their Christianity is not superficial adherence but a deeply implanted moral and spiritual formation. The next 100 years in Africa will be as significant, or more so, than the 20th century has so evidently been for African Christianity.

Pentecostalism and the charismatic movement
A 20th-century movement that has grown in almost African proportions has been worldwide Pentecostalism. As a denomination, Pentecostals look back to the Azusa Street Revival in Los Angeles, California of 1906 as a point of departure. A black revivalist, William J. Seymour, who had been shaped by Wesleyan teaching on holiness, began to teach a 'baptism of the Spirit', associated with speaking in tongues as evidence of it. One immediate result, surprising in its day, was that blacks, Hispanics and white Americans were found worshipping together in Azusa Street between 1906 and 1909. From these small beginnings, the movement spread to Canada, South America, Scandinavia, England and Germany. Today, analysts divide the movement into Pentecostals (a denomination), charismatics (those in mainline denominations) and neo-charismatics (groups formed since 1980 outside mainline denominations).

Since 1960, there has been much growth of the movement in the traditional denominations, termed the charismatic movement. Charismatics are found in Roman Catholicism, Anglicanism, Lutheranism and other mainline churches. Of all the areas of the world, Latin America has been the scene of the greatest development. Of the 60 million members of the churches who see themselves as sharing in the charismatic renewal, 33 million are in the Latin American countries. In Chile, some 36 per cent of all Christians are reckoned to be Pentecostal, charismatic or neo-charismatic. The proportions are similar in Colombia (30 per cent) and Argentina (22 per cent). The country with the strongest presence, however, is Brazil, where one recent estimate, possibly inflated, gives a figure of 47 per cent of all Christians in the three categories; the strength of the Assemblies of God (Pentecostal Churches) alone is said to contain 100,000 pastors and 500,000 recognized lay leaders. Even if the figure of 79 million in all three

St Peter's basilica, during the inauguration of the Ecumenical Council. More than 2700 church leaders came to Rome from all over the world to attend the council.

categories is exaggerated, it indicates a movement of very large numbers. The third category of neo-charismatics is a sign, as among the African Independent Churches mentioned earlier, that indigenous forms of Christianity, which bear comparison to the first two groupings with their emphasis on healing, prophecy and exuberant worship with speaking in tongues, have sprung up as independent, non-denominational expressions of local Christianity.

A new centre of gravity

These figures are a reminder of the shift in Christian population from the predominance of the north (Europe and North America) to the south in the 20th century. In 1900 the overwhelming number of Christians were in the

Vatican II (1963–65)

Regarded by many as the most significant religious event of the 20th century, the Second Vatican Council was summoned by Pope John XXIII (1883–1963; pope from 1958) who was over 80 years of age when it met. He gave the council the task of renewal (*aggiornamento*) of the life of the church. It was attended by 2,300 bishops from all over the world, of whom 800 came from the younger churches of Asia, Africa and Oceania. Observers from the Orthodox, Anglican and other churches were also invited. It ushered in an immense process of adjustment for the Roman Catholic church. A predominant view of the church as 'the people of God' in movement, rather than as a static and hierarchical institution, issued in vernacular (rather than Latin) liturgies, an emphasis on collegiality and shared ministry among bishops, a permanent and married diaconate (though celibacy remained the rule for priests) and a greater openness to the 'separated brethren' of the non-Roman churches.

'A complete change in the centre of gravity of Christianity [has occurred] so that the heartlands of the Church are... in Latin America... parts of Asia and... in Africa.'

ANDREW WALLS,
EMERITUS
PROFESSOR OF
UNIVERSITY OF
EDINBURGH

so-called 'sending' countries of the missionary era. Now, the balance has shifted to Africa, south of the Sahara, Latin America and the Pacific in a proportion of 60–40; put another way, if Christians are estimated at two billion of a world population of six billion, well over half of these are to be found in the south, in what were traditionally regarded as the 'mission fields'. Further large numbers of missionaries, intent on expanding the influence of the Christian gospel in often post-Christian lands, are to be found in nations such as South Korea (which has around 10,000 missionaries, of whom some hundreds are to be found in Japan, Russia and the Philippines) and Nigeria, which has over 3,000 missionaries. Although there is still pioneering work to do by such bodies as Wycliffe Bible Translators (founded in 1934), among peoples whose languages have yet to be expressed in written forms and into which the Bible has yet to be translated, the main ethnic groups have been evangelized over two millennia in terms of territorial outreach. The Christian churches are confronted with a different, if no less challenging, task.

In the 20th century, Christianity has faced the challenge of an aggressively atheistic alternative in Communism, lasting in Europe in its Marxist–Leninist form from the Russian revolution of 1917 until the fall of the Berlin Wall in 1989. It has faced also the challenge of neo-pagan Aryan Nazism. The Dutch missionary thinker, Hendrik Kraemer, regarded both as modern 'tribalisms', offering the security of false religions and false absolutes, securities that are also sought by many in the different forms of fundamentalism, religious or otherwise, in the contemporary world. The century has seen much profound reflection on Christian expansion. This was true of the World Missionary Conference at Edinburgh in 1910, even if its optimism would now seem excessive, and of the conferences mounted by the International Missionary Council (which resulted from Edinburgh) and led to analyses of the world scene in Jerusalem in 1928 and Tamabaram, Madras in 1938. It was for this meeting that Kraemer wrote his explosive preparatory volume *The Christian Message in a Non-Christian World*. Since 1950, the documents of the Second Vatican Council have provided highly stimulating reflection on the church's task in *Ad Gentes* (the decree on the Church's Missionary Activity 'to the nations'), *Lumen Gentium* (the dogmatic constitution on the Church as 'the Light of the Nations') and *Nostra Aetate* (the declaration of the relation of the Church to non-Christian religions 'in our age'). Pope John Paul II's recent calls for re-evangelization build on one of his predecessor's reminders of 1975 that evangelization is the church's essential function 'inherent in the very nature of the church', which itself needs to be evangelized before 'carrying forth... the good news to every sector of the human race' for its renewal and transformation (Pope Paul VI in *Evangelii Nuntiandi*). Much valuable material for reflection can also be found in the documents of the Lausanne Congress on World Evangelization of 1974, mounted by evangelicals.

In a changed world and changed context, when, as Paul VI discerned, there is a rift between the gospel and a secularized modern culture, the emphasis on witness remains valid. Luke's words at the beginning of this story 'you will be my witnesses... to the ends of the earth' remain as true as ever, even in the light of two millennia of territorial expansion of the Christian faith.

'The age of missions is at an end; the age of mission has begun.'

STEPHEN NEILL,
A HISTORY OF CHRISTIAN MISSIONS

Chronology

26–36: Pontius Pilate's governorship in Judea.

c. 30: crucifixion of Jesus of Nazareth.

51: Paul appears before Gallio in Corinth.

64: Nero blames the fire of Rome on Christians. Probable date of Mark's Gospel.

c. 107: Martyrdom of Ignatius, bishop of Antioch, in Rome.

112: Pliny the younger's correspondence with Emperor Trajan about Christians.

312: Constantine's victory at Milvian Bridge.

c. 340: Frumentius in Ethiopia as a Christian.

386: Augustine of Hippo's experience in the garden in Milan.

410: Alaric the Goth sacks Rome.

c. 529: Benedict founds the monastery at Monte Cassino.

563: Columba founds the monastery on Iona.

596: Gregory I (Pope) sends Augustine to Canterbury.

635: Alopen reaches China. Aidan evangelizes Northumbria.

c. 696: Lindisfarne Gospels.

754: Boniface is martyred at Dokkum.

800: Charlemagne is crowned emperor in Rome; possible date of *Book of Kells*

830: Anskar founds church in Sweden (Stockholm).

910: Monastery at Cluny founded.

c. 988: Vladimir baptized in Kiev.

1098: Cistercian Abbey founded at Citeaux.

1130: Chartres Cathedral begun.

1209: Francis founds order by permission of Innocent III.

1216–8: Dominic founds order.

1415: Jan Hus is burned.

1483: Portuguese in Kongo; African king baptized (1491).

1492: Columbus's voyage of discovery.

1493: Papal bull *Ceteris Partibus* divides world between Spain/Portugal.

1498: Vasco da Gama sails to India.

1520: Cortes destroys Aztec capital and founds Mexico City.

1540: Francis Xavier (Jesuit) to Goa (dies in 1552 off China).

1550: Bartholemew de las Casas debates Indian rights at Valladolid.

1583: Jesuits into China.

1600: East India Company founded.

1614: Jesuits expelled from Japan (entered 1542).

1622: Propaganda Fidei founded in Rome.

1701: Society for the Propagation of the Gospel founded (SPG).

1706: Ziegenbalg and Plütschau to India as first Protestant missionaries.

1739: Moravian community of Genadendal founded in South Africa by G. Schmidt.

1742: David Brainerd begins work among native Americans.

1769: Captain Cook visits Tahiti.

1773: Suppression of the Jesuit Order.

1792: William Carey to India: foundation of the Baptist Missionary Society.

1795: London Missionary Society founded. LMS voyage of *Duff* (1796).

1799: Church Missionary Society (CMS) founded.

1810: American Board of Commissioners for Foreign Missions founded.

1814: Samuel Marsden preaches first Christian sermon in New Zealand.

1815: Basel Missionary Society founded. Society of Mary (Marists) founded (1816).

1839: John Williams martyred on Erromanga, New Hebrides.

1841: Father Chanel martyred on Futuna.

1853–56: David Livingstone's trans-continental journeys in central Africa.

1857: Indian Mutiny (Sepoy rebellion). British Government assumes rule.

1858: Treaty of Tientsin opens interior of China to western influence.

1865: China Inland Mission (CIM) founded by James Hudson Taylor.

1871: John Patteson martyred on Nukapu.

1892: Mangena Mokone founds the 'Ethiopian Church of South Africa'.

1901: James Chalmers is martyred in New Guinea.

1903: Zionist Apostolic Church is founded in Zululand.

1906–9: Azusa Street Revival in Los Angeles: birth of modern Pentecostalism.

1910: Edinburgh World Missionary Conference.

1912: Prophet Harris's campaigns in West Africa.

1921: Simon Kimbangu imprisoned in Belgian Congo.

1952: President Nkrumah head of state in Ghana.

1963–65: Second Vatican Council in Rome.

1974: Lausanne Congress on World Evangelization.

1977: Archbishop Janani Luwum martyred in Uganda.

1990: Nelson Mandela is freed in South Africa.

Suggestions for Further Reading

General overviews

J. Combey, *How to Understand the History of Christian Mission*, SCM Press, 1996.

K.S. Latourette, *A History of the Expansion of Christianity* (7 vols), Harper and Row, 1971.

Stephen Neill, *A History of Christian Missions* revised edition, Penguin, 1986.

Africa

Adrian Hastings, *The Church in Africa 1450–1950*, Oxford University Press, 1994.

E. Isichei, *A History of Christianity in Africa*, SPCK, 1995.

B.G.M. Sundkler and C. Steed, *A History of the Church in Africa*, Cambridge University Press, 2000.

Asia

S.H. Moffett, *A History of Christianity in Asia: Beginnings to 1500*, Orbis, 1998.

S. Sundquist (ed.), *A Dictionary of Asian Christianity*, Eerdmans, 2001.

Latin America

E. Dussel (ed.), *The Church in Latin America 1492–1992*, Burns and Oates, 1992.

Oceania

I. Breward, *A History of the Churches of Australasia*, Oxford University Press, 2001.

C.W. Forman, *The Island Churches of the South Pacific*, Orbis, 1982.

Special studies

David Bosch, *Transforming Mission*, Orbis, 1991.

A. Harnack, *The Mission and Expansion of Christianity*, tr. J. Moffatt, Harper, 1904.

Andrew Ross, *A Vision Betrayed: The Jesuits in Japan 1542–1742*, Edinburgh University Press, 1994.

Andrew Ross, *David Livingstone: Mission and Empire*, Hambledon and London, 2002.

Andrew Walls, *The Missionary Movement in Christian History*, T & T Clark, 1996.

Timothy Yates, *Christian Mission in the Twentieth Century*, Cambridge University Press, 1994.

Useful reference works

G.H. Anderson (ed.), *Biographical Dictionary of Christian Missions*, Simon & Schuster, 1998.

David Barrett (ed.), *World Christian Encyclopedia* (2 vols), Oxford University Press, 2001.

T. Dowley (ed.), *The Atlas of the Bible and the History of Christianity*, British and Foreign Bible Society, 1997.

S.C. Neill, G.H. Anderson and J. Goodwin, *A Concise Dictionary of the Christian World Mission*, Lutterworth Press, 1970.

Larger church dictionaries

F.L. Cross and E.A. Livingstone, *The Oxford Dictionary of the Christian Church*, 3rd edition, Oxford University Press, 1997.

New Catholic Encyclopedia (15 vols), McGraw-Hill, 1967.

Index

Picture and Text Acknowledgments

Pictures

Picture research by Zooid Pictures Limited.

AKG – Images: pp. 10 (Erich Lessing), 17, 42–43 (Bibliothèque Nationale), 93, 111, 112.

Alexander Turnbull Library, Wellington, New Zealand: p. 151.

Ancient Art & Architecture: p. 45 (Ronald Sheridan).

Baptist World Mission Archive, Regent's Park College, Oxford: p. 141.

Bridgeman Art Library: pp. 39 (National Palace Museum, Taipei, Taiwan), 89 (Peter Willi/Chateau de Beauregard, France), 96–97 (Hotel de Dieu Collections, Quebec, Canada), 100–101 (Phillips, The International Art Auctioneers).

British Museum: p. 24.

Church Mission Society: p. 175.

Circa Photo Library: pp. 36–37 (Xia Ju Xian).

Corbis UK Ltd: pp. 1 (Lowell Georgia), 2–3 (David Muench), 6–7 (Marc Garanger), 12 (Archivo Iconografico, S.A.), 13 (Archivo Iconografico, S.A.), 18–19 (Benjamin Rondel), 30–31 (Roger Wood), 46 (Philip Gould), 48–49 (Adam Woolfitt), 54 (Archivo Iconografico, S.A.), 57 (Josè F. Poblete), 63 (Archivo Iconografico, S.A.), 70–71 (Carmen Redondo), 79 (Stapleton Collection), 102, 109, 114–15 (Archivo Iconografico, S.A.), 117 (Bettmann), 119 (Bettmann), 125 (Leonard de Selva), 130 (Bettmann), 157 (Francis G. Mayer), 162 (Bettmann), 166–67 (Kraft Brooks/Sygma), 168–69 (Daniel Lainè), 178 (Bettmann), 180–81 (Bettmann).

DEFAP – Service Protestant de Mission: p. 84.

Dundee Central Library: p. 76.

Genadendal Mission Museum: p. 77.

Jasper Jacob Associates: p. 28.

Mary Evans Picture Library: pp. 4–5, 120, 136, 147.

Eileen McGuckin: p. 15.

National Library of Australia: pp. 148–49 (by permission).

OMF International: p. 140.

The Royal Collection © 2003, Her Majesty Queen Elizabeth II: p. 128.

Werner Forman Archive: 126–27 (Art Institute, Chicago).

Derek West: maps on pp. 20–21, 26–27, 34–35, 51, 64, 81, 91, 104–105, 134–35, 154–55, 171.

White Fathers: p. 83.

Text

Scripture quotations are from the New Revised Standard Version published by HarperCollins Publishers, copyright © 1989 by the Division of Christian Education of the National Council of the Churches of Christ in the USA, and are used by permission. All rights reserved.

Lion Publishing

Commissioning editor: Morag Reeve

Project editor: Olwen Turchetta

Designer: Nicholas Rous

Production manager: Kylie Ord